# DO

## ON SOME ASPECTS OF
# EVANGELIZATION

### CONGREGATION FOR THE
### DOCTRINE OF THE FAITH

PAULIST PRESS
New York / Mahwah, NJ

Cover photograph by Benjamin Haas/Shutterstock.com.
Cover design by Sharyn Banks
Book design by Lynn Else

Library of Congress Cataloging-in-Publication Data

Catholic Church. Congregatio pro Doctrina Fidei.
   Doctrinal note on some aspects of evangelization / Congregation for the Doctrine of the Faith.
      p. cm.
   Includes bibliographical references (p.      ).
   ISBN 978-0-8091-4760-1 (alk. paper)
   1. Evangelistic work—Catholic Church. 2. Catholic Church—Missions.
3. Evangelistic work—Papal documents. 4. Missions—Papal documents.
5. Catholic Church—Doctrines. I. Title.
   BX2347.4.C368 2012
   269'.2—dc23
                                                            2012004035

Published by Paulist Press
997 Macarthur Boulevard
Mahwah, New Jersey 07430

www.paulistpress.com

Printed and bound in the United States of America

# CONTENTS

iii

# Contents

# FOREWORD

William Cardinal Levada
Prefect,
Congregation for the Doctrine of the Faith

---

"So that God may be all in all"

(1 Corinthians 15:28)

The Congregation for the Doctrine of the Faith is pleased to present its *Doctrinal Note on Some Aspects of Evangelization*. This doctrinal note addresses a central theme of the Catholic and Christian understanding of our believing in Jesus Christ, the theme of evangelization. As Jesus was sent by the Father to bear the good news of salvation, so he enjoined his disciples to proclaim the good news—the gospel—to all the entire world and to all the nations. This work, this deed of evangelization, appertains to the authentic nature of the Church. As Christians have received this great gift of God's love in Christ, naturally they have the wish—indeed, the duty—to share it with their own families, friends, and neighbors.

Why a document on evangelization? From their conversations with the bishops of the world, and from an analysis of a certain confusion regarding the question of whether Catholics have a duty to give witness of their own faith in Christ, the Congregation has indicated certain issues that seem to prejudice the execution of Christ's missionary mandate, and so has recalled three basic points in this regard, corresponding to three implications of evangelization.

The anthropological implications of evangelization concern two key factors in human existence: freedom and truth. It is the conviction of Christian faith that the revelation of God, of the divine love for us in Christ, leads humanity toward the truth of God's intention and of the divine plan of creation and redemption. Knowledge of this truth is a blessing for humanity and for every single human being. At the same time, human dignity demands that the quest for such truth respect the freedom of the human conscience. Only one as great as Saint Paul might not hesitate to describe conversion to the Christian faith as liberation, [since] fully belonging to Christ, who is Truth, and entering the Church do not lessen human freedom but rather exalt it and direct it toward its fulfillment (*Note*, 7). Consequently, evangelization must never resort to "coercion or tactics unworthy of the Gospel" (*Note*, 8). At the same time, religious freedom imposes the obligation of seeing to it that evangelization not meet with restrictive obstacles calculated to inhibit its function or expansion.

The ecclesiological implications of the *Doctrinal Note* remind us: "Since the day of Pentecost...the Gospel, in the power of the Spirit, is proclaimed to all people, so that they might believe and become disciples of Christ and members of his Church....Conversion...signifies a change in thinking and in acting, as the expression of the new life *in Christ*." For Christian evangelization, "the incorporation of new members into the Church is not the expansion of a power-group, but rather entrance into the network of friendship with Christ which connects heaven and earth, different continents and ages....The Church, therefore, is the bearer of the presence of God and thus the instrument of the true humanization of man and the world" (*Note*, 9). Finally, the importance of the Christian witness of holiness and of charity is essential for the credibility of evangelization.

In addressing the ecumenical implications, the *Doctrinal Note* takes a position in the furrow of the modern ecumenical movement, whose origins, at the beginning of the past century, are due in large measure to the concerns of the Christian missioners who saw their missionary effort frustrated by the multiple, competing, existing church structures. The work of evangelization among the Christians of varying confessions leads to dialogue, and to the sharing of gifts that promote a more profound conversion to Christ. When, however, individual persons decide in conscience to adhere to the Catholic Church, these decisions should be respected without accusing the Catholic Church of a negative approach to proselytism.

The *Doctrinal Note* concludes with a beautiful citation from the first Encyclical Letter of Pope Benedict XVI: "The love coming from God joins us to Him, and transforms ourselves into a 'We,' that defeats our divisions and makes us to be one single thing, that God at last be 'all in all' (1 Cor 15:28)." I sincerely hope that this document may be an instrument of renewal in the deed and work of evangelization of Catholics and of all Christians, and a guideline for the unification of the siblings of the entire human family.

# PREFACE

## The Joy and the Duty of Proclaiming the Truth of Christ

Evangelization is a fundamental duty of the Church and of the Christian. After his resurrection, Jesus sent his apostles into the whole world, to proclaim "the good news to the whole creation" (Mark 16:15; cf. Matt 28:19–20). With this document, *Doctrinal Note on Some Aspects of Evangelization*, significantly dated December 3, 2007, Feast of Saint Francis Xavier, Patron of the Missions, the Congregation for the Doctrine of the Faith seeks emphatically to restate the vital importance that evangelization has for the life of the Church and to remind all of their duty to proclaim Christ to those who as yet do not know him.

This *Doctrinal Note*, which presupposes the teaching of Pope Paul VI and Pope John Paul II, who have amply treated the subject of evangelization, is intended as a clarification of certain particular aspects of the rapport between the missionary mandate of the Lord and respect for the conscience and religious freedom of all (*Note*, 3).

Following a brief "Introduction" (Part I, 1–3), the theme is developed in the central chapters, which treat, respectively, certain anthropological (Part II, 4–8), ecclesiological (Part III, 9–11), and ecumenical (Part IV, 12) implications. A brief "Conclusion" (Part V, 13) closes the exposition. We shall not enter into an examination of the individual points that have been treated in the "Introduction" of Cardinal William Levada, or of the relevant theological contributions that follow, but shall be satisfied merely with a few indications.

First and foremost, we observe that the document underscores the fact that the human being has received the divine gifts of intellect and will in order to be able to love God freely, as well as to see that the desire to make one's gifts known and to share them with others is a deep anthropological reality; that one who has discovered the truth of Christ feels impelled to communicate it to others, so that they too may be able to become sharers of this gladness, gratuitously and lovingly to bestow on others what one has gratuitously received.

The ecclesiological implications that derive from these facts are clear. In the Church and by way of the Church, God is made present in the world. And mission becomes a service to this presence of God by way of the reign of God, a reign that cannot be separated from the Church. Respect for freedom of religion, which is always observed, cannot, however, be transformed into indifference to truth and good. The apostolic task is necessary for the life of the Church. It is a matter of an assignment that comports, surely, with a public proclamation of the gospel, but also with a personal witness not belied by one's personal conduct. The proclamation and a consistency of life with the same must go ever hand in hand.

Also important are certain precisions regarding the ecumenical dimension of evangelization. Collaboration, and sincere respect for the traditions of non-Catholic Christians, must hinder neither a presentation of the plenitude of the Catholic faith to Christians of other confessions who are freely disposed, without coercion from any quarter, to its acceptance, nor the gladsome welcome of one who requests to enter into full communion with the Catholic Church.

In its "Conclusion," the document strongly reemphasizes that relativism—supreme today in certain milieus—will never constitute a valid motive for any neglect of the duty to evangelize, which is the essential task of the Church. May the Lord grant that this *Doctrinal Note*, published by the Congregation for the Doctrine of the Faith, may contribute to the arousal of all Catholics, in the respective state and vocation of each, to an ever keener experience of the joy and the duty of letting everyone know the good news of Christ.

Archbishop Luis Ladaria
*Secretary*
Congregation for the Doctrine
of the Faith

# PART 1
# DOCUMENT

# DOCTRINAL NOTE ON SOME ASPECTS OF EVANGELIZATION

## I. INTRODUCTION

1. Jesus Christ was sent by the Father to proclaim the Gospel, calling all people to conversion and faith (cf. Mark 1:14–15). After his resurrection, he entrusted the continuation of his mission of evangelization to the Apostles (cf. Matt 28:19–20; Mark 16:15; Luke 24:4–7; Acts 1:3): "As the Father has sent me, so I send you" (John 20:21; cf. 17:18). By means of the Church, Christ wants to be present in every historical epoch, every place on earth and every sector of society, in order to reach every person, so that there may be one flock and one shepherd (cf. John 10:16): "Go into all the world and proclaim the good news to the whole creation. The one who believes and is baptized will be saved; but the one who does not believe will be condemned" (Mark 16:15–16).

The Apostles, therefore, "prompted by the Spirit, invited all to change their lives, to be converted and to be baptized,"[1] because the "pilgrim Church is necessary for salvation."[2] It is the same Lord Jesus Christ who, present in his Church, goes before the work of evangelizers, accompanies

3

it, follows it, and makes their labors bear fruit: what took place at the origins of Christian history continues throughout its entire course.

At the beginning of the third millennium, the call which Peter and his brother Andrew, as well as the other first disciples, heard from Jesus continues to resound in the world: "put out into the deep and let down your nets for a catch" (Luke 5:4).[3] And after the miracle of a huge catch of fish, the Lord revealed to Peter that he would become "a fisher of men" (cf. Luke 5:10).

2. The term *evangelization* has a very rich meaning.[4] In the broad sense, it sums up the Church's entire mission: her whole life consists in accomplishing the *traditio Evangelii*, the proclamation and handing on of the Gospel, which is "the power of God for salvation to everyone who has faith" (Rom 1:16) and which, in the final essence, is identified with Jesus Christ himself (cf. 1 Cor 1:24). Understood in this way, evangelization is aimed at all of humanity. In any case, *to evangelize* does not mean simply to teach a doctrine, but to proclaim Jesus Christ by one's words and actions, that is, to make oneself an instrument of his presence and action in the world.

"Every person has the right to hear the 'Good News' of the God who reveals and gives himself in Christ, so that each one can live out in its fullness his or her proper calling."[5] It [is] a right which the Lord himself confers on every person, so that every man and woman is able truly to say with Saint Paul: Jesus Christ "loved me and gave himself for me" (Gal 2:20). This right implies the corresponding duty to evangelize: "If I proclaim the gospel, this gives me no ground for boasting, for an obligation is laid on me, and woe betide me if I do not proclaim the gospel" (1 Cor 9:16; cf. Rom 10:14). Thus, it is evident how every activity of the Church has an essential evangelizing dimension and must never be separated from the commitment to help all persons to meet Christ in faith, which is the primary objective of evangelization: "Social issues and the Gospel are inseparable. When we bring people only knowledge, ability, technical competence and tools, we bring them too little."[6]

3. There is today, however, a growing confusion which leads many to leave the missionary command of the Lord unheard and ineffective (cf. Matt 28:19). Often it is maintained that any attempt to convince others on religious matters is a limitation of their freedom. From this perspective, it would only be legitimate to present one's own ideas and to invite people to act according to their consciences, without aiming at their conversion to Christ and to the Catholic faith. It is enough, so they say, to help people to become more human or more faithful to their own religion; it is enough to build communities which strive for justice, freedom, peace and solidarity. Furthermore, some maintain that Christ should not be proclaimed to those who do not know him, nor should joining the Church be promoted, since it would also be possible to be saved without explicit knowledge of Christ and without formal incorporation in the Church.

In the face of these problems, the Congregation for the Doctrine of the Faith has judged it necessary to publish the present *Note*. This document, which presupposes the entirety of Catholic doctrine on evangelization, as extensively treated in the teaching of Paul VI and John Paul II, is intended to clarify certain aspects of the relationship between the missionary command of the Lord and respect for the conscience and religious freedom of all people. It is an issue with important anthropological, ecclesiological and ecumenical implications.

# II. SOME ANTHROPOLOGICAL IMPLICATIONS

4. "This is eternal life, that they may know you, the only true God and Jesus Christ whom you have sent" (John 17:3). God has given human beings intellect and will so that they might freely seek, know and love him. Therefore, human freedom is both a resource and a challenge offered to man by God who has created him: an offer directed to the human person's capacity to know and to love what is good and true. Nothing puts in play human freedom like the search for the good and the true, by inviting it to a kind of commitment which involves fundamental aspects of life. This is particularly the case with salvific truth, which is not only an object of thought, but also an event which encompasses the entire person—intelligence, will, feelings, actions and future plans—when a person adheres to Christ. In the search for the good and the true, the Holy Spirit is already at work, opening the human heart and making it

ready to welcome the truth of the Gospel, as Thomas Aquinas stated in his celebrated phrase: *omne verum a quocumque dicatur a Spiritu Sancto est.*[7] It is important therefore to appreciate this action of the Spirit, who creates an affinity for the truth and draws the human heart towards it, by helping human knowledge to mature both in wisdom and in trusting abandonment to what is true.[8]

Today, however, with ever-increasing frequency, questions are being raised about the legitimacy of presenting to others—so that they might in turn accept it—that which is held to be true for oneself. Often this is seen as an infringement of other people's freedom. Such a vision of human freedom, separated from its integral reference to truth, is one of the expressions "of that relativism which, recognizing nothing as definitive, leaves as the ultimate criterion only the self with its desires and under the semblance of freedom, becomes a prison for each one."[9] In the various forms of agnosticism and relativism present in contemporary thought, "a legitimate plurality of positions has yielded to an undifferentiated pluralism, based upon the assumption that all positions are equally valid, which is one of today's most widespread symptoms of the lack of confidence in truth. Even certain conceptions of life coming from the East betray this lack of confidence, denying truth its exclusive character and assuming that truth reveals itself equally in different doctrines, even if they contradict one another."[10] If man denies his fundamental capacity for the truth, if he becomes skeptical regarding his ability really to

7

know what is true, he ends up losing what in a unique way draws his intelligence and enthralls his heart.

5. In this connection, when it comes to the search for truth, whoever trusts only in his own individual efforts and does not recognize the need for help from others, is deceiving himself. Human beings "from birth, therefore, are immersed in traditions which give them not only a language and a cultural formation but also a range of truths in which they believe almost instinctively....Nonetheless, there are in the life of a human being many more truths which are simply believed than truths which are acquired by way of personal verification."[11] The need to trust in the knowledge handed on by one's culture or acquired by others, enriches a person with truths that could not have been attained on one's own, as well as by the interpersonal and social relationships which this process develops. Spiritual individualism, on the other hand, isolates a person, hindering him from opening in trust to others—so as both to receive and to bestow the abundant goods which nourish his freedom—and jeopardizes the right to manifest one's own convictions and opinions in society.[12]

In particular, the truth which is capable of shedding light on the meaning of one's life and giving it direction, is similarly attained through trusting acceptance with regard to those persons who are able to guarantee the certainty and authenticity of the truth itself: "There is no doubt that the capacity to entrust oneself and one's life to another person and the decision to do so are among the most significant and expressive human acts."[13] Although it happens on a deeper level, the acceptance of revelation which takes place through faith also falls within the dynamics of the search for truth: "'The obedience of faith' (Rom 16:26; cf. Rom 1:5; 2 Cor 10:5–6) must be given to God who reveals; by this obedience of faith man freely commits his entire self to God, offering 'the full submission of intellect and will to God who reveals' and freely assenting to the revelation given by him."[14] The Second Vatican Council, after having affirmed the right and the duty of every person to seek the truth in matters of religion adds: "The search for truth, however, must be carried out in a manner that is appropriate to the dignity of the human person and his social nature, namely, by free enquiry with the help of teaching or instruction, communication and dialogue. It is by these means that people share with each other the truth they have discovered, or think they have discovered, in such a way that they help one another in the search for truth."[15] In any case, the truth "does not impose itself except by the strength of the truth itself."[16] Therefore, to lead a person's intelligence and freedom in honesty to the encounter with Christ and his Gospel is not an inappropriate encroachment, but rather a legitimate endeavor and a service capable of making human relationships more fruitful.

6. Evangelization does not only entail the possibility of enrichment for those who are evangelized; it is also an enrichment for the one who does the evangelizing, as well as for the entire Church. For example, in the process of inculturation, "the universal Church herself is enriched with forms of expression and values in the various sectors

of Christian life....She comes to know and to express better the mystery of Christ, all the while being motivated to continual renewal."[17] Indeed, since the day of Pentecost, the Church has manifested the universality of her mission, welcoming in Christ the countless riches of peoples from all times and places in human history.[18] Beyond its intrinsic anthropological value, every encounter with another person or culture is capable of revealing potentialities of the Gospel which hitherto may not have been fully explicit and which will enrich the life of Christians and the Church. Thanks to this dynamism, "tradition, which comes from the Apostles, makes progress in the Church by the help of the Holy Spirit."[19]

It is indeed the Holy Spirit who, after having been operative in the incarnation of Jesus Christ in the womb of the Blessed Virgin Mary, animates the maternal action of the Church in the evangelization of cultures. Although the Gospel is independent from any culture, it is capable of infusing all cultures, while never allowing itself to be subservient to them.[20] In this sense, the Holy Spirit is also the principal agent of the inculturation of the Gospel, presiding in a fruitful way at the dialogue between the Word of God, revealed in Christ, and the deepest questions which arise among the multitude of human beings and cultures. In this way, the Pentecost-event continues in history, in the unity of one and the same faith, enriched by the diversity of languages and cultures.

7. The communication of religiously significant events and truths in order that they will be accepted by

others is not only in profound harmony with the human phenomena of dialogue, proclamation and education; it also corresponds to another important anthropological fact: the desire, which is proper to the human person, to have others share in one's own goods. The acceptance of the Good News in faith is thus dynamically ordered to such a communication. The truth which saves one's life inflames the heart of the one who has received it with a love of neighbor that motivates him to pass on to others in freedom what he has freely been given.

Although non-Christians can be saved through the grace which God bestows in "ways known to him,"[21] the Church cannot fail to recognize that such persons are lacking a tremendous benefit in this world: to know the true face of God and the friendship of Jesus Christ, God-with-us. Indeed "there is nothing more beautiful than to be surprised by the Gospel, by the encounter with Christ. There is nothing more beautiful than to know him and to speak to others of our friendship with him."[22] The revelation of the fundamental truths[23] about God, about the human person and the world, is a great good for every human person, while living in darkness without the truths about ultimate questions is an evil and is often at the root of suffering and slavery which can at times be grievous. This is why Saint Paul does not hesitate to describe conversion to the Christian faith as liberation "from the power of darkness" and entrance into "the kingdom of his beloved Son in whom we have redemption, the forgiveness of sins" (Col 1:13–14). Therefore, fully belonging to Christ, who is the

Truth, and entering the Church do not lessen human freedom, but rather exalt it and direct it towards its fulfillment, in a love that is freely given and which overflows with care for the good of all people. It is an inestimable benefit to live within the universal embrace of the friends of God which flows from communion in the life-giving flesh of his Son, to receive from him the certainty of forgiveness of sins and to live in the love that is born of faith. The Church wants everyone to share in these goods so that they may possess the fullness of truth and the fullness of the means of salvation, in order "to obtain the freedom of the glory of the children of God" (Rom 8:21).

8. Evangelization also involves a sincere dialogue that seeks to understand the reasons and feelings of others. Indeed, the heart of another person can only be approached in freedom, in love and in dialogue, in such a manner that the word which is spoken is not simply offered, but also truly witnessed in the hearts of those to whom it is addressed. This requires taking into account the hopes, sufferings and concrete situations of those with whom one is in dialogue. Precisely in this way, people of good will open their hearts more freely and share their spiritual and religious experiences in all sincerity. This experience of sharing, a characteristic of true friendship, is a valuable occasion for witnessing and for Christian proclamation.

As in any other field of human activity, so too in dialogue on religious matters, sin can enter in. It may sometimes happen that such a dialogue is not guided by its natural purpose, but gives way instead to deception, selfish motives or arrogance, thus failing in respect for the dignity and religious freedom of the partners in dialogue. For this reason, "the Church severely prohibits forcing people to embrace the faith or leading or enticing them by improper techniques; by the same token, she also strongly defends the right that no one be deterred from the faith by deplorable ill treatment."[24]

The primary motive of evangelization is the love of Christ for the eternal salvation of all. The sole desire of authentic evangelizers is to bestow freely what they themselves have freely received: "From the very origins of the Church, the disciples of Christ strove to convert men to faith in Christ the Lord; not, however, through coercion or tactics unworthy of the Gospel, but above all by the power of the word of God."[25] The mission of the Apostles and its continuation in the mission of the early Church remain the foundational model of evangelization for all time: it is a mission that has often been marked by martyrdom, as demonstrated by the history of the twentieth century. It is precisely martyrdom that gives credibility to witnesses, who seek neither power nor advantage, but instead lay down their lives for Christ. Before all the world, they display an unarmed strength brimming with love for all people, which is bestowed on those who follow Christ unto the total gift of their existence. So it is that Christians, from the very dawn of Christianity up until our own time, have suffered persecution on account of the

Gospel, as Jesus himself foretold: "If they persecuted me, they will also persecute you" (John 15:20).

# III. SOME ECCLESIOLOGICAL
# IMPLICATIONS

9. Since the day of Pentecost, one who fully accepts the faith is incorporated into the community of believers: "those who welcomed his message [Peter's] were baptized and that day about three thousand persons were added [to them]" (Acts 2:41). Since the beginning, the Gospel, in the power of the Spirit, is proclaimed to all people so that they might believe and become disciples of Christ and members of his Church. In the writings of the Fathers of the Church, there are constant exhortations to fulfill the mission entrusted by Christ to his disciples.[26] Generally, the term *conversion* is used in reference to bringing pagans into the Church. However, conversion (*metanoia*), in its precisely Christian meaning, signifies a change in thinking and in acting, as the expression of the new life *in Christ* proclaimed by faith: a continuous reform of thought and deeds directed at an ever more intense identification with Christ (cf. Gal 2:20), to which the baptized are called before all else. This is, in the first place, the meaning of the call made by Jesus himself: "repent and believe in the good news" (Mark 1:15; cf. Matt 4:17).

The Christian spirit has always been animated by a passion to lead all humanity to Christ in the Church. The incorporation of new members into the Church is not the expansion of a power-group, but rather entrance into the network of friendship with Christ which connects heaven and earth, different continents and ages. It is entrance into the gift of communion with Christ, which is "new life" enlivened by charity and the commitment to justice. The Church is the instrument, "the seed and the beginning"[27] of the Kingdom of God; she is not a political utopia. She is already the presence of God in history and she carries in herself the true future, the definitive future in which God will be "all in all" (1 Cor 15:28); she is a necessary presence, because only God can bring authentic peace and justice to the world. The Kingdom of God is not—as some maintain today—a generic reality above all religious experiences and traditions, to which they tend as a universal and indistinct communion of all those who seek God, but it is, before all else, a person with a name and a face: Jesus of Nazareth, the image of the unseen God.[28] Therefore, every free movement of the human heart towards God and towards his kingdom cannot but by its very nature lead to Christ and be oriented towards entrance into his Church, the efficacious sign of that Kingdom. The Church, therefore, is the bearer of the presence of God and thus the instrument of the true humanization of man and the world. The growth of the Church in history, which results from missionary activity, is at the service of the presence of God through *his* Kingdom: one cannot in fact "detach the Kingdom from the Church."[29]

10. However, the Church's "missionary proclamation is endangered today by relativistic theories which seek to

justify religious pluralism, not only *de facto* but also *de iure* (or in principle)."[30] For a long time, the reason for evangelization has not been clear to many among the Catholic faithful.[31] It is even stated that the claim to have received the gift of the fullness of God's revelation masks an attitude of intolerance and a danger to peace.

Those who make such claims are overlooking the fact that the fullness of the gift of truth, which God makes by revealing himself to man, respects the freedom which he himself created as an indelible mark of human nature: a freedom which is not indifference, but which is rather directed towards truth. This kind of respect is a requirement of the Catholic faith itself and of the love of Christ; it is a constitutive element of evangelization and, therefore, a good which is to be promoted inseparably with the commitment to making the fullness of salvation, which God offers to the human race in the Church, known and freely embraced.

Respect for religious freedom[32] and its promotion "must not in any way make us indifferent towards truth and goodness. Indeed, love impels the followers of Christ to proclaim to all the truth which saves."[33] Such love is the sign of the authentic presence of the Holy Spirit who, as the principal agent of evangelization,[34] never ceases to move people's hearts when they hear the Gospel, by opening them to receive it. It is a love which lives in the heart of the Church and from there, as burning charity, radiates out to the ends of the earth, as far as the heart of every human being. The entire heart of man awaits the encounter with Jesus Christ.

Thus one understands the urgency of Christ's invitation to evangelization and why it is that the mission entrusted by the Lord to the Apostles involves all the baptized. The words of Jesus "go therefore and make disciples of all nations, baptizing them in the name of the Father and of the Son and of the Holy Spirit, and teaching them to obey everything that I have commanded you" (Matt 28:19–20), are directed to everyone in the Church, each according to his own vocation. At the present time, with so many people in the world living in different types of *desert*, above all, in the "desert of God's darkness, the emptiness of souls no longer aware of their dignity or the goal of human life,"[35] Pope Benedict XVI has recalled to the world that "the Church as a whole and all her Pastors, like Christ, must set out to lead people out of the desert, towards the place of life, towards friendship with the Son of God, towards the One who gives us life, and life in abundance."[36] This apostolic commitment is an inalienable right and duty, an expression of religious liberty, with its corresponding ethical-social and ethical-political dimensions.[37] It is a right which in some parts of the world, unfortunately, has not yet been recognized and which in others is not respected in practice.[38]

11. He who announces the Gospel participates in the charity of Christ, who loved us and gave himself up for us (cf. Eph 5:2); he is his ambassador and he pleads in the name of Christ: let yourselves to be reconciled with God! (cf. 2 Cor 5:20). It is a charity which is an expression of the gratitude that flows from the heart when it opens to the love given in Jesus Christ, that Love which, as Dante

wrote, is displayed throughout the universe.[39] This explains the ardor, the confidence, and the freedom of speech (*parrhesia*) evident in the preaching of the Apostles (cf. Acts 4:31; 9:27–28; 26:26, etc.) and which Agrippa experienced when he heard Paul speaking: "You are so quickly persuading me to become a Christian!" (Acts 26:28).

Evangelization is not only accomplished through public preaching of the Gospel nor solely through works of public relevance, but also by means of personal witness which is always very effective in spreading the Gospel. Indeed, "side by side with the collective proclamation of the Gospel, the other form of handing it on, from person to person, remains valid and important.…It must not happen that the pressing need to proclaim the Good News to the multitudes should cause us to forget this form of proclamation whereby an individual's personal conscience is reached and touched by an entirely unique word that he receives from someone else."[40]

In any case, it needs to be remembered that, in transmitting the Gospel, word and witness of life go together.[41] Above all, the witness of holiness is necessary, if the light of truth is to reach all human beings. If the word is contradicted by behavior, its acceptance will be difficult. However, even witness by itself is not enough "because even the finest witness will prove ineffective in the long run, if it is not explained, justified—what Peter called 'giving a reason for the hope that is in you' (1 Pet 3:15)—and made explicit by a clear and unequivocal proclamation of the Lord Jesus."[42]

# IV. SOME ECUMENICAL IMPLICATIONS

12. From its beginnings, the ecumenical movement has been closely connected with evangelization. Unity, in fact, is the seal of the credibility of missionary activity and so the Second Vatican Council noted with regret that the scandal of division "damages the most sacred cause of preaching."[43] Jesus himself, on the night before his death, prayed "that they may all be one…so that the world may believe" (John 17:21).

The mission of the Church is universal and is not restricted to specific regions of the earth. Evangelization, however, is undertaken differently according to the different situations in which it occurs. In its precise sense, *evangelization* is the *missio ad gentes* directed to those who do not know Christ. In a wider sense, it is used to describe ordinary pastoral work, while the phrase "new evangelization" designates pastoral outreach to those who no longer practice the Christian faith.[44] In addition, there is evangelization in countries where non-Catholic Christians live, including those with an ancient Christian tradition and culture. In this context, what is required is both true respect for the tradition and spiritual riches of such countries as well as a sincere spirit of cooperation. Catholics, "avoiding every form of indifferentism or confusion, as well as senseless rivalry, through a common profession of faith in God and in Jesus Christ before all peoples—insofar as this is possible—may collaborate with their separated brethren in social, cultural, technical and religious matters in accordance with the Decree on Ecumenism."[45]

Different dimensions of the work of ecumenism can be distinguished: above all, there is *listening*, as a fundamental condition for any dialogue, then, *theological discussion*, in which, by seeking to understand the beliefs, traditions and convictions of others, agreement can be found, at times hidden under disagreement. Inseparably united with this is another essential dimension of the ecumenical commitment: *witness and proclamation* of elements which are not particular traditions or theological subtleties, but which belong rather to the Tradition of the faith itself.

Ecumenism does not have only an institutional dimension aimed at "making the partial communion existing between Christians grow towards full communion in truth and charity."[46] It is also the task of every member of the faithful, above all by means of prayer, penance, study and cooperation. Everywhere and always, each Catholic has the right and the duty to give the witness and the full proclamation of his faith. With non-Catholic Christians, Catholics must enter into a respectful dialogue of charity and truth, a dialogue which is not only an exchange of ideas, but also of gifts,[47] in order that the fullness of the means of salvation can be offered to one's partners in dialogue.[48] In this way, they are led to an ever deeper conversion to Christ.

In this connection, it needs also to be recalled that if a non-Catholic Christian, for reasons of conscience and having been convinced of Catholic truth, asks to enter into the full communion of the Catholic Church, this is to be respected as the work of the Holy Spirit and as an expression of freedom of conscience and of religion. In such a case, it would not be a question of proselytism in the negative sense that has been attributed to this term.[49] As explicitly recognized in the Decree on Ecumenism of the Second Vatican Council, "it is evident that the work of preparing and reconciling those individuals who desire full Catholic communion is of its nature distinct from ecumenical action, but there is no opposition between the two, since both proceed from the marvelous ways of God."[50] Therefore, the work of ecumenism does not remove the right or take away the responsibility of proclaiming in fullness the Catholic faith to other Christians, who freely wish to receive it.

This perspective naturally requires the avoidance of any undue pressure: "in spreading religious faith and introducing religious practices, everyone should refrain at all times from any kind of action which might seem to suggest coercion or dishonest or improper persuasion, especially when dealing with poor or uneducated people."[51] The witness to the truth does not seek to impose anything by force, neither by coercive action nor by tactics incompatible with the Gospel. By definition, the exercise of charity is free.[52] Love and witnessing to the truth are aimed above all at convincing others through the power of the word of God (Cf. 1 Cor 2:3-5; 1 Thess 2:3-5).[53] The Christian mission resides in the power of the Holy Spirit and in the truth itself which is proclaimed.

# V. Conclusion

13. The Church's commitment to evangelization can never be lacking, since according to his own promise, the presence of the Lord Jesus in the power of the Holy Spirit will never be absent from her: "I am with you always, to the end of the age" (Matt 28:20). The relativism and irenicism prevalent today in the area of religion are not valid reasons for failing to respond to the difficult, but awe-inspiring commitment which belongs to the nature of the Church herself and is indeed the Church's "primary task."[54] "*Caritas Christi urget nos*—the love of Christ urges us on" (2 Cor 5:14): the lives of innumerable Catholics bear witness to this truth. Throughout the entire history of the Church, people motivated by the love of Jesus have undertaken initiatives and works of every kind in order to proclaim the Gospel to the entire world and in all sectors of society, as a perennial reminder and invitation to every Christian generation to fulfill with generosity the mandate of Christ. Therefore, as Pope Benedict XVI recalls, "the proclamation of and witness to the Gospel are the first service that Christians can render to every person and to the entire human race, called as they are to communicate to all God's love, which was fully manifested in Jesus Christ, the one Redeemer of the world."[55] The love which

comes from God unites us to him and "makes us a 'we' which transcends our divisions and makes us one, until in the end God is 'all in all' (1 Cor 15:28)."[56]

*The Sovereign Pontiff Benedict XVI, in the Audience granted to the undersigned Cardinal Prefect on 6 October 2007, approved the present* Doctrinal Note, *adopted in the Ordinary Session of this Congregation, and ordered its publication.*

*Rome, from the Offices of the Congregation for the Doctrine of the Faith, 3 December 2007, Memorial of Saint Francis Xavier, Patron of the Missions.*

William Cardinal Levada
*Prefect*

Angelo Amato, SDB
*Titular Archbishop of Sila*
*Secretary*

# PART 2
# COMMENTS

# THE ANTHROPOLOGICAL PRESUPPOSITIONS OF THE CHRISTIAN MESSAGE

Javier María Prades López

"And this is eternal life, that they may know you, the only true God, and Jesus Christ whom you have sent" (John 17:3). Jesus' solemn assertion recapitulates the proper nature of evangelization as the proposal of an enduring life (see Congregation for the Doctrine of the Faith, *Doctrinal Note on Some Aspects of Evangelization*, 4). Eternal life is the fullness of existence, by virtue of a participation in the divine life—a fullness as earnestly desired as it is unattainable by our own powers. In order to obtain happiness, in this life and everlastingly, it is not enough for us human beings to know that there is a real God, a "true God," simply in a quite impersonal sense. We need to meet this God, personally, in the place and period of our life story. And this is possible, thanks to the incarnation, and to its sacramental prolongation in the Church, that is, thanks to the meeting with Christ, in which is life (cf. John 1:4). We human persons attain to the life that truly is life, that is, when, through the gift of the Holy Spirit, we lovingly recognize and acknowledge Jesus as the Son, sent from the Father that we "may have life, and have it to the full" (John 10:10). The happy destiny of every person is therefore linked to the two great dogmatic mysteries of our faith, to which Saint John alludes: the Trinity and the incarnation.

The mission and task of proposing this full life are frequently abandoned, by reason of a situation of confusion, which the *Doctrinal Note* identifies by a number of factors. Among the latter, the two principal ones are (1) the reduction of the Christian message to the promotion of merely human values (justice, freedom, peace, solidarity, and so on) and (2) the relativism that separates freedom from a reference to truth. When this mentality is interiorized, evangelization is renounced, for fear that the proposition of the gospel becomes an "unwarranted interference" with, or even "an attack on the freedom" of the interlocutor (cf. *Note*, 3–4). Given the seriousness of these consequences, the *Doctrinal Note* examines the anthropological presuppositions of the like objections and confronts them with the correct concept of the human being in the light of revelation, not only in order to answer the accusation but also to demonstrate that evangelization is a boon, a legitimate service that renders human beings' interrelationships more fertile (*Note*, 5).

The presupposition of a rational superiority of certain values in the face of the historical fact, along with a defense of cultural relativism, are two criteria that condition the matter of understanding the relationships between cultures and religions. These criteria have their roots in Western illuministic modernity and continue today to exercise a considerable influence in the debate concerning multiculturalism. This is the context of thought in which the evangelizing mission is at stake. The first step, then, in an anthropological survey will consist in a delineation, however brief, of the pair of factors cited above.

The rationalistic mentality postulated that rational and ethical universality was superior to the religious traditions precisely because it abstracted from any historical particularity. The positive religions were not strictly universal—and therefore must not be public—whereas the culture of modernity, which made of the state the guarantor of citizens' rights and liberties, did indeed enjoy that universality, with the citizen now being deprived of any identity. Accordingly, the state was elevated to the status of guarantor of the religions, and these now reduced to purely private phenomena of conscience.

In many currents of contemporary multiculturalism that bear the post-illuministic label, the difficulty is radicalized. Not only are religious traditions not restored their universal value, but reason itself is deprived of it (exception being made for its deconstructive power). No longer is there universal reason or culture, but only particular "reasons" or "cultures." Not only the religions but all of the cosmovisions lose their universal, or authentic, character. The cultural and religious identities, respectively, are merely juxtaposed, excluding any possibility of establishing between them a true rational or ethical confrontation (cf. *Note*, 4).

Multiculturalism stresses the public value of particular identities and rejects the modern universalistic conception because it regards it as precisely owing to its abstraction. For its own part, universalism of an illuministic matrix champions the equality of the human condition. To that end, universalism formalizes the human condition abstractly in determinate ethical and juridico-political contents and/or procedures, incapable of respecting whatever is typical of each respective culture (the citizen is universal as such, but there is no community identity), and rejects what it considers the fragmentation of identities as a wellspring of arbitrariness. Each of these tendencies, which share the same presuppositions, criticizes the other because they are two "unsatisfied" expressions of a deeper need that they fail to meet: the need for a recognition and an acknowledgment of a cultural oneness in which universality and particularity are not reciprocally exclusive. Both illuministic universalism and post-illuministic multiculturalism eviscerate the Christian aspiration, as is to be observed in the theological models that absorb these influences and relativize evangelization (cf. *Note*, 3).

According to these currents, if the Christian faith is but one religio-cultural variant among others, and if we possess no criteria of universal confrontation, then there is no rational alternative but to renounce its universal proposition. Christianity—like any other philosophy, culture, or religion—would be deprived of legitimate title reasonably to address the freedom of the other. Now each individual will stay shut up in a private cultural and religious world. Excluded will be not only any proposition to the other of one's own experience but also dialogue itself among human persons—indeed the very capacity to communicate verbally at all (cf. *Note*, 10). Nor would a solution be reached with the reduction of the Christian faith to a set of ethical or social values, detached from their historical origin in the Christ event (as we find documented in the ethical Christianity of illuminism, in which this reduction is frequently offered).

Let us see in what way, instead, an original Christian experience can propose a convincing synthesis between these two cultural attitudes (public value of particular identity, and equality of all human beings), at the same time overcoming their respective drawbacks (cultural relativism and abstract universalism). Christianity would be a reasonable proposition for anyone, once it was presented in terms of the actual nature of its dogmatic mysteries, without homologizing it with any cultural conception (cf. *Fides et ratio*, 70ff.; *Note*, 6).

Revelation identifies the human being constitutively as *imago Dei* (cf. Gen 1:26–27). Why does this conceptualization of the human being, understood in the light of the Trinity and of the incarnation, supply adequate foundation for the universal proposition of a particular fact? To put it another way: how is it reasonable to assert that the destiny of the everlasting happiness of all (universal value)

depends on the individual's encounter with Jesus Christ—
a particular fact? An approach to these questions *in extenso*
would carry us into the classic consideration of the relationship between Christology and anthropology. Here we
restrict ourselves to placing in evidence certain assertions
relative to Part 2 of the *Doctrinal Note*.

*Gaudium et spes* no. 22 has become the programmatic
enunciation of the relationship between the human mystery and that of the Incarnate Word. Thanks to the conciliar renewal, theological anthropology sets in sharp relief
the christological mediation of the created (cf. *Gaudium et
spes*, 10–12), with special emphasis on who the human
person is in the Pauline assertion concerning the two
Adams (Rom 5:14; 1 Cor 15:45ff.), with its ample com-
mentary at the hands of the first Christian theologians
(Irenaeus, Tertullian). This anthropology teaches that the
complete truth of the humanity of Jesus, being that of the
Son of God (in its dimensions of predestination, incarnation, and redemption of the human being), springs from the
event of Jesus Christ, the human being corresponding to
God absolutely and the definitive image of the Father (Col
1:15; 2 Cor 4:4). The singular humanity of Jesus, being the
humanity of the Son of God, implies a determination of all
that is to be human as valid for all human beings. And in
this sense its aspiration is universal (cf. *Note*, 9).

In this way, a dogmatic foundation is available for a
universal action of evangelization. Each human being is
God's image, not in any generic modality, as if he or she
were but one "natural" creature among others—no, this

creature's creation is historically oriented toward the mysteries of the Trinity and the incarnation. Each one of us has been loved by the Father once and for all as the image of the Incarnate Son, in whose image alone our humanity can be completed. It does not suffice, therefore, that we know there to be a true God, a real God; we must encounter in history the One who is the definitive image of the Father and the perfect human being (cf. *Note*, 7), participating in the communion of the divine life by way of membership in the Church, and definitively in heaven.

Christian revelation manifests its novelty only when it attributes to the history of Jesus of Nazareth the character of event of the free communication of the Triune God (cf. *Dei Verbum*, 2, 4; *Deus caritas est*, 1, 12). God's truth has been revealed in the free obedience of Jesus of Nazareth, and this is why the manifestation of transcendent truth has willed to involve human freedom. This is the case with the free response of Jesus, and also the case, however, with the Christian's free response to revelation (as Mary's "Be it done unto me" constitutes such response"!). Faith makes up part of revelation, since the latter is always attested (whether by the Son, or by the "sons [and daughters] of the Son," through the mediation of the Holy Spirit), and thereby acquires a decisive weight for an understanding of the bond between anthropology and Christology (cf. *Note*, 5).

It is therefore intrinsic to the Christ event to safeguard the consistency and relative autonomy of the human as an internal dimension of revelation. Thus, evangeliza-

33

tion translates into act the human being's capacity for truth, exalting the irreplaceable value of freedom. In such a way, a recognition of the method of God's revelation as the transcendent causation of some particular historical event entails a recognition of the truth of historical experience: we now see that historical facts are not to be abandoned if we want to penetrate to their ultimate foundation. To say it another way: it is not necessary to conceptualize the transcendence of universal Truth outside the relationship of freedom with its concrete, historical conditions. Thanks to this defense, typifying the Christian proclamation, of the intimate rapport between historical condition ("flesh") and Mystery of God ("Word"), the particular circumstance is invested with an irreducible value (and so we welcome what is true in multiculturalism), precisely because it can render present universal truth (aspiration of the modern illuminist), defeating the aporia between historical relativism and abstract universalism from which Western culture fails to emerge. Only if we evangelize shall we open the West to the opportunity to reconcile with itself (cf. *Note*, 13).

The *Doctrinal Note* recalls that salvific truth "is not only an object of thought, but also an event which encompasses the entire person—intelligence, will, actions and future plans—when a person adheres to Christ" (4).

The characterization of truth as an event involving the entire person offers the foundation for an understanding of the correct relationship between reason and freedom. This dynamism is proper to the quest for truth at all of the levels of life; and so it also occurs, through the gift of the Holy Spirit, in the reception of revelation (cf. *Note*, 5). Bearing testimony to himself even through the created (cf. *Dei Verbum*, 3), God arouses an attraction that impels creation's subjects to know him as Creator by way of his works and deeds. In fact, one who seeks transcendent truth is always factually situated within creation and history. To accede to truth, he or she must always live the concrete circumstances of reality, which kindles an initial surprise, and a rational dynamism takes hold that does not let go at the first correspondent but seeks to go "on and on," so as to arrive at the mysterious origin of all of those circumstances. This movement implicates all of the dimensions of the person, which knows itself, the world, and God the more, the deeper it steeps itself in realities (cf. *Fides et ratio*, 1). The enrichment of the person, then, is produced in the measure that she or he lives an intense relationship with reality, and not when it remains in a voluntarily neutral indifference in the face of the real.

We understand, then, why human beings can and should open out to others in all trust, especially to those who best escort them into this relationship with the Mystery that creates all things. This dynamism of reason, with freedom toward God, which identifies with creaturely dependency, discloses the loftiest dignity of everyone. It does not, however, manage to be definitive, since neither the (finite) other, nor the sum-total of all others, can bring it about that the personal relationship with God win unique, non-transferable traits (cf. *Gaudium et spes*, 19–21). In order for this latter condition to supervene, it is further needed that there materialize a historical experience with the Absolute, who addresses the freedom of the person and enunciates her or his name. Each of us has been able fully to discover the mysterious and non-reiterable signification of our "I," in virtue of a particular event befalling us in our life story. It is the Jesus Christ event that bestows fullness upon the mystery of our freedom: God has entered our history as a real factor in order to challenge our freedom, personalizing it in a way that can never be repeated (baptism and vocation). We manage to know ourselves to the extent that we accept the "filiation" conferred on us as a form of our life, and so freely discover the good foundation of our existence. Adhesion to the filial form of Christ, in the Holy Spirit, renders responsibility in the life of earth more acute. That is, the more we discover the filial signification of our existence, the more we are impelled to exercise our capacity of adhesion and decision in all the ambits of personal and social life. Once it is established that the existence of Jesus Christ culminates in the acceptance of the Father's will, as he puts at stake the whole truth of his "I," and so exposing his divine filiation, every one of ourselves is offered the opportunity of participating in this singular form of filiation, thanks to which we are able to reach that "stature / maturity of Christ" (Eph 4:13). Once this becomes reality, we shall be participating by grace, in the eternal glory of the Triune God.

The second part of the *Doctrinal Note* concludes with the indication that method of evangelization, in the ambit of sincere dialogue with human beings, consists in the witness/testimony and proclamation (cf. *Note*, 8), in the likeness of Jesus Christ, the faithful and truthful Witness (cf. Rev 3:14). The one who knows everlasting life, the one who knows the true God and Jesus Christ whom he has sent, experiences the beauty of "full life," which satisfies reason and freedom. The person who has this experience, and who lives it, this unheard-of enrichment of his or her personality (cf. *Note*, 6) grows in the desire to communicate it to others (cf. *Note*, 7). Only in this manner, by way of the communication of a superabundant gift—is conferred the sole possible implementation of the right of all to receive this good news (cf. *Note*, 2). How could one find an event more consonant with the being of all, both more personal and of larger public projection—more particular and more universal?

# THE ECCLESIOLOGICAL PRESUPPOSITIONS OF EVANGELIZATION

Alberto Cozzi

---

In every communicative act, the communicator *anticipates* somehow *an ideal community*, that is, expresses and interprets bonds, relationships, and thus also, rights and duties. The Church, communicating the gospel of Jesus Christ, anticipates as ideal community the trinitarian communion: "Thus the universal Church presents herself as 'a people united in the oneness of the Father, the Son, and the Holy Spirit'" (*Lumen gentium*, 4). Jesus says in his priestly prayer: "The glory that you have given me I have given them, so that they may be one, as we are one, I in them and you in me, that they may become completely one, so that the world may know that you have sent me and have loved them even as you have loved me" (John 17:22–23).

What does it mean that, in their proclamation of the gospel, Christians bear a gift that not only does not constrain their brother or sister but creates new ties in which one attains to communion with very God? "We declare to you what we have seen and heard so that you also may have fellowship with us; and truly our fellowship is with the Father and with his Son Jesus Christ" (1 John 1:3). In this text, one clearly sees how the proclamation of what has been experienced in the encounter with Christ is, in the concrete, an extension of the bonds of communion created by a new community, at whose origin is the communion of Father and Son. This same certainty is powerfully expressed in the key texts of Vatican II, cited in *Dominus Iesus*: "On the one hand, 'the Church is a sacrament, that is, a sign and instrument of intimate oneness with God, and of the oneness of the human race' (*Lumen gentium*, 1). She is sign and instrument of the Reign, then—summoned to proclaim and establish it. On the other hand, the Church is the 'people united in the oneness of the Father, the Son, and the Holy Spirit' (*Lumen gentium*, 4). Therefore she is 'the Reign of Christ already present in mystery' (*Lumen gentium*, 3)."[1]

With regard to this original certainty of Christian faith, *Doctrinal Note on Some Aspects of Evangelization* (December 3, 2007) places in evidence, at the ecclesiological level, three possible crises against which we ought to be on our guard: a "crisis of membership," of "belonging" (9); a "crisis of pretended truth" (10); and a "crisis of testimonial" to an experience (11). It is a matter of uncertainties and doubts that cloud the consciousness of the evangelizing task of Jesus' disciples precisely because they obscure a perception of the missionary nature of the Church.

1. The first crisis, brought into focus by no. 9 of the

*Doctrinal Note*, regards the sense of "membership" in the Church. The problematic to be "read between the lines" is that of the pretended defeat of an "ecclesiocentric" logic: in its work, its activity of evangelization, the Church must resist the temptation to flaunt itself, in order to concentrate on the proclamation of Jesus Christ and his reign.[2]

According to this sensibility, it remains the case that the Church ought to proclaim, since it is in the service of the universal salvific activity of God, but it ought not proclaim itself. Rather it ought to "dissolve," in the salvific action of God in favor of human beings.[3] Granted, a mentality of this type runs the risk of forgetting that the ideal community, anticipated in each communicative act, cannot be without a "body," that is, without real bonds, historically effective and measurable. In this sense, the community created ought to be inserted in concrete history, and in a people joined in the fetters of faith, ritual deeds and gestures (sacraments), and (apostolic) tradition. Here, in the crisis of the sense of belonging, of membership, one is aware of a double crisis: that of bonds or connections, and that of presence. In the crisis of bonds or links, there is often present ingenuous reading of the gratuity of the gift of the gospel: we announce it, "proclaim" it, without imposing ourselves on others. But does this also mean "proclaiming" it without creating bonds, without offering ourselves to communion, to friendship? In order to correct this crisis of historical, concrete bonds, the *Doctrinal Note* offers the beautiful image of incorporation into the Church as "entrance into the network of the friendship with Christ which connects heaven and earth, different continents and ages" (9). In the effort of evangelization, it is not a matter of extending a power group animated by some political utopia or other; no, this is entry into the gift of communion with Christ, which is new life animated by the love of charity and a commitment to justice. As for the "crisis of presence," which tends to separate the Church from Christ, and therefore from the reign, as if the Christian community were not the Body of Christ, in which is realized a new salvific presence of God, the *Doctrinal Note* insists that the Church "is already the presence of God in history…a necessary presence, because God alone can bring authentic peace and justice to the world" (9).[4] The evangelizing Church is the vehicle of "the presence of God and thus the instrument of the true humanization of man and the world" (9). Therefore, the Church is not a pure function of a universal and anonymous salvific action of God, without a proper consistency, but is a network of links and bonds in which is realized the presence of God who saves. And here we recover the original, positive sense of the axiom *extra ecclesiam nulla salus*: the Church has been endowed by God with all of the salvific gifts and means for the attainment of truth and life.[5]

2. The second crisis cited by the *Doctrinal Note* (10) derives from the recent forms of pluralistic relativism. It is the "crisis of a pretense of truth"—the crisis of a false or unrealistic claim to truth. One can "read between the lines" of this claim the reduction of the Church to a partial cultural function alongside other cultural forms. As such, the

Church ought not to burden truth with its own viewpoint, from the moment that, and simply because, an individual single culture is not identified with universal truth. Accordingly, it is not authorized to announce or proclaim its truth to others in order to convert them: to do so might well wound their liberty of conscience. Instead, it ought to limit itself to "dialoguing" with other cultures and religions. Over and above a problematical reduction of freedom to "indifference in confrontations with truth and the good" to which the *Doctrinal Note* explicitly alludes, there now arises as well the danger of losing the true sense of Church through a flawed conception of culture and its relationship to the truth of the human being. The very fact is interesting that the pluralistic mentality, particularly in the recent theology of the religions, should have formulated the interrelationship with the religions as a problem of the relationship between "Christianity and the religions," neglecting the Church, which is actually the concrete historical subject of these relations. Indeed, the notion of "Christianity" actually runs the risk of reducing the faith to a certain cultural form. To the account of a like mentality is to be laid, on the one hand, a reductive notion of culture and, on the other, a misperception of the cultural dimensions of belonging to the Church. A help to correct these erroneous conceptions is to be had in a pair of considerations offered by theologian Joseph Ratzinger. The first regards the dynamic meaning of culture and its openness to the universality of truth.

The various cultures live not only their own experience of God, the world, and the human being. Along their pathway they inevitably meet with other cultural subjects, and these must be confronted with the sometimes very different experiences of others. Therefore the moment of their opening up or sealing fast their attitudes is the moment when the deepening and purification of one's own knowledge and evaluations can occur. This can lead to a profound transformation of the form of the prevailing cultural model. The prospect of a positive transformation depends on the potential universality of any given culture, as concretized in an acceptance of what is another's, and a change in what is one's own.[6]

At bottom, the meeting of cultures is possible because the human person, despite all of the differences in her and his history and communitarian creations, is one identical and unique being. This unique being that is the human person, in the depth of his and her existence, can come to be "intercepted" by truth itself. This is what produces a dynamic and communicative vision of the cultures, which testifies to the typical openness of human beings to the universal and to transcendence: "Accordingly, as expressions of the single human essence, the cultures are characterized by the precious human dynamic which transcends all erstwhile limits."[7] In the light of these considerations, one can gather—and here Ratzinger's second consideration comes operative—the relation between faith and culture. The means that places the one in contact with the other can only be the human person's common truth, in which what is at issue is the truth about God and reality in its entire complex. The more a culture is

conformable to human nature—the more elevated it is—
the more it aspires to the truth that, up to a certain point, it
had been excluded from, and all the more readily will it be
able to come into immediate contact with such truth, and
to assimilate it. This being said, it suddenly occurs to adjoin
that the Church is a cultural subject, even while it is not a
matter of one particular culture, the Church being a people
composed of the union of so many peoples. There is no such
thing as a pure faith in the sense that it would be without
cultural mediation. Therefore, the Christian can have a
double culture, that of origin and that of faith. To believe
means to enter a people, the Church, with its one culture
and its one history. But how can Christianity be a culture
without being a particular one? It is possible to maintain
both assertions in the presence of the transcendence of cultures in the Bible and in the history of the faith.

> All peoples are invited to enter into this process
> of the defeat of particularity, which has had its
> commencement first and foremost in Israel, in
> its turning to that God who has outdone him-
> self in Jesus Christ, and has broken down the
> wall of hostility between us (Eph 2:12) and is
> escorting us toward one another in the expro-
> priation of himself that was accomplished on
> the cross. Faith in Jesus Christ, accordingly, is a
> continuous opening, irruption [*Einbruch*] of
> God into the human world and an opening
> [*Aufbruch*] of the human person in response to

God, who at the same time leads human beings toward one another. Everything that belongs to us now belongs to everyone, and everything that is the others' now becomes ours too.[8]

Faith has brought the peoples close not to a particular culture but to the dynamic of victory over self for the sake of an approach to the universal truth of the human person, who constitutes the authentic point of impact for the interpretation of the Christian message. The exodus, the cultural fracture, with its dying in order to be reborn, is a basic trait of Christianity.

No one is born Christian, not even in a Christian world and of Christian progenitors. Christianity can arrive always and only as new birth. In the notion of revelation the "unowned," that which does not belong to my own sphere, approaches me and bears me up, away from myself, beyond myself. Something new carries us within a larger space, and precisely in this way…opens us up to the opportunity to come side by side with one another.[9]

This invitation to the exodus, to the flight to a greater truth, which faith propitiates, echoes in the *Doctrinal Note*, when the duty is recalled of each Christian to evangelize, taking the road "to lead people out of the desert, towards the place of life, towards friendship with

God, towards the One who gives us life, life in abundance" (10). It would seem that the best answer to certain forms of pluralistic relativism would be a loud call to duty, a mighty summons to accompany human beings on the exodus to the "ever greater truth" and therefore universal, to which we are called by God.

3. The third form of the crisis of evangelization is identified in the *Doctrinal Note* (11) as a "crisis of personal testimonial" to an experience. In the first Letter of John, cited above, this apostle offers the idea of a contagious experience, sparked by a joy uncontainable, a gladness that cannot be reserved just for ourselves. The *Doctrinal Note* speaks in the sense of a "gratitude for the love given in Christ" and inserted in the dynamics of this bestowal, and earmarked for every human being. The gospel is communication of a love that opens to others. It is incumbent on the evangelizer to feel this communication of love, and so to "get involved." We are at the level of personal testimonial, of encounter and exchange. We are "person to person." Our notification is not to be cheapened, as too often happens, by being conveyed as a public, solemn announcement, after the fashion of a proclamation, forgetting the importance of a personal transmission of the faith, which continues to constitute the authentic texture of the evangelizing act of the Christian communities. One need only recall the capillary deed performed in Christian initiation in the parishes, or, of course, of family education in faith and prayer. It is worth one's while, then, to recall the essential "interpersonal dimension" of evangelization, in

which the Church is confirmed as a concrete historical community, made of personal bonds and faces. The *Doctrinal Note* does so by incorporating a beautiful text of Pope Paul VI, to be found in his Apostolic Exhortation *Evangelii nuntiandi* (46), which reads: "Side by side with the collective proclamation of the Gospel, the other form of transmission, the person-to-person one, remains valid and important....It must not happen that the pressing need to proclaim the Good News to the multitudes should cause us to forget this form of proclamation whereby an individual's personal conscience is reached and touched by an entirely unique world that he receives from someone else."

The evangelizing Church is not just some anonymous cultural group engaged in defending its particular viewpoint on reality. She is a living community, made of concrete historical ties and animated by a living presence of God, in Christ, and which, by personal contact, opens wide the power of the love of God that creates communion.

# CONCLUSION

The ecclesiological presuppositions of evangelization call for the acknowledgment of a twofold impossibility: the impossibility of diluting the Church into a partial aspect of God's action in favor of human beings, on the one hand, and, on the other, the impossibility of considering that Church as an independent reality in itself, disconnected from its relationship to Christ. In the first regard here, we have received the enlightening image of the Church as a marriage partner, a spouse (cf. Eph 5:25–30), and therefore a reality of her own, standing, by gift and call, before Christ at her consigned place.

In the second respect, the Church is to be thought of as Christ's body (cf. 1 Cor 12:12–27), in which is realized his presence, that germ and instrument of the reign in history. The image of *spouse* complements that of *body*, announcing that she is not diluted into merely an intermediate subject of God's action for the benefit of the world. No, she is the extension of the work and deed of Christ, and a subject stationed before him, woven of real bonds and actual faces, receiving and realizing the new communion of the Father and the Son. The image of the body illumines that of the spouse, recalling that the Church stands before Christ not as an autonomous reality, "preconstituted" vis-à-vis its gift and station—instead, she is the fruit of the radical bestowal and engagement of herself, which Christ has accomplished in his Passover. The Church is set by Christ before himself as his immaculate spouse, summoned to a free response of love. Her evangelizing assignment and commitment consist precisely of involving persons in this identical response of love, by way of such closely knit concrete bonds in which is realized the presence of Christ in his body.

# EVANGELIZATION, NEW EVANGELIZATION, AND MISSION "AD GENTES"

## Bishop Antonio Staglianò

The gospel is always the announcement of hope for all, in every place and at every time. In its quality as "good news," the gospel is a communication of salvation, a response to every human demand, explicit or implicit. "Yesterday, today, and always," Christ is the same. His mystery is inexhaustible, in "breadth, height, length, and depth." Every age, every culture, can expect to find in the gospel of Christ the needed "wisdom" (= *Logos*) to guide life along the path of truth, justice, love, solidarity, and community in peace.

Evangelization is not, then, "a" task of the Church. It is a roaring blaze of mission afire in the world, burning to say "yes" to the human freedom to meet with Christ's salvation just as Christ himself encounters every human being. The recent *Doctrinal Note on Some Aspects of Evangelization* lays hold of this concept: "The term *evange-*

*lization* has a very rich meaning. In the broad sense, it sums up the Church's entire mission: her whole life consists in accomplishing the *traditio Evangelii*, the proclamation and handing on of the Gospel" (2). In his Apostolic Exhortation *Evangelii nuntiandi*, Pope Paul VI had already written, "Evangelizing is in fact the grace and vocation proper to the Church, her deepest identity. She exists in order to evangelize" (14).

## EVANGELIZATION "IS" CHURCH

Evangelization, then, is the actual purpose for which the Church exists. For that matter, inasmuch as Christian faith has a performative dimension, and not merely an informative one, the meeting with the gospel—as Pope Benedict XVI teaches authoritatively in his Encyclical Letter *Spe salvi* (10)—"molds life itself in a new way," indeed, transforms and supports the everyday. Further, "The Gospel is not only a communication of things that can be known, but is a communication that produces facts and changes life" (2). Thus, the existence of the community of believers, in itself, appears as a concrete example of what is meant by "the inculturation of the Gospel"—namely, evangelization itself, in the many forms of Christian testimonial, visible and public. In other words, it must be shown "how and how much" the preaching of the gospel generates *ethos*, behavior, lifestyles. Scant danger, then, in the fact that evangelization leads to the Church! True, it leads to belonging to it—in profound depth and lively attitude. The Congregation's *Doctrinal Note* makes it clear: "The incorporation of new members into the Church is not the expansion of a power-group, but rather entrance into the network of friendship with Christ which connects heaven and earth, different continents and ages" (9). Indeed, by her very constitution, the Church lives the great mystery of her indissoluble union with Christ by the divine will: "The two will become one flesh. This is a great mystery, and I am applying it to Christ and the Church" (Eph 5:31–32).

Thus, mysteriously, to bear Christ to the world as a declaration of its salvation takes on the genuine meaning of a truthful ecclesial self-presentation. If the Church "says anything" to the world, she can only say herself. Immunized, however, from a destructive narcissism, she "says" herself as the reality whose plenitude of content is the Word, which she obeys, and of which she is the function, the lowly, humble sign—frequently opaque, but ever real. Church symbolical: sacrament of a Reality that is her Foundation, and that limitlessly exceeds her. Church doxological: intrinsically facing the Father in adoration, of whom she pronounces the face, with a voice, a "saying," that existentially exhausts her, for she does not *have* but *is* this speech, this address—by and in this all, Church ineluctably extrovert.

# THE NEED FOR A "NEW EVANGELIZATION"

The commission of evangelization calls for permanent attention to the evolution of the peoples and the nations, in order to be enfleshed and proactive in the spaces of people's lives, in society, family, occupation, and culture. Therefore, in the face of hedonism, consumerism, religious indifferentism, relativism and moral laxity, libertarianism, and cultural and practical materialism—which disorient believers living in today's society—a profound meaning and prophetic intuition accrue to Pope John Paul II's summons to the "new evangelization."

In his Apostolic Exhortation *Christifideles laici*, the same Pope John Paul very clearly delineates the task and its motivation:

> Whole countries and nations where religion and the Christian life were formerly flourishing and capable of fostering a viable and working community of faith, are now put to a hard test, and in some cases, are even undergoing a radical transformation, as a result of a constant spreading of an indifference to religion, of secularism and atheism. This particularly concerns countries and nations of the so-called First World, in which economic well-being and consumerism, even if coexistent with a tragic situation of poverty and misery, inspires and sustains

54

a life lived "as if God did not exist." This indifference to religion and the practice of religion devoid of true meaning in the face of life's very serious problems, are not less worrying and upsetting when compared with declared atheism. (34)

Thus, the Congregation's *Doctrinal Note* (12) readily distinguishes among "evangelization" ("ordinary pastoral work"), "new evangelization" (pastoral outreach "to those who no longer practice the Christian faith"), "evangelization" that is *"missio ad gentes* directed to those who do not know Christ," and finally, "evangelization in countries where non-Catholic Christians live, including those with an ancient Christian tradition and culture." In sum, while evangelization remains homogeneous and one, still it is diversified in respect the persons to whom it is directed. For all of the forms of evangelization, however, the pair of conditions holds good that John Paul indicates for the authenticity of the "new evangelization": *a new ardor, and a new awareness of Christian truth.* The conditions, as it happens, are mutually interior. The ardor is born of a certitude that Christian truth is a good for the one who receives it for the first time as for the one who recovers it when it has been lost. It is the ardor of the one who knows his or her deed to be positive, to have been accomplished not to destroy but to build, to edify, for there is no incompatibility between the gospel and cultures. And so, even the new awareness bears on the fact that Christian truth is not simply a doctrine to explain but a piece of good news, charged with hope for existence, and, as such, not imposed violently but testimonially—that is, charged as well with one's own liberty, in love and ardor for one's proclamation. *Christian truth is Christ himself in his person*—God Crucified, who does not impose, but who attracts, with his openness to the gift of himself, all the way to the extremity of death—"death on the cross," as salvation and liberation, justice, human community in peace and charity.

# THE GOSPEL CORRESPONDING TO THE FULLNESS OF HUMAN LIFE

Rightly, the *Doctrinal Note* insists on showing how the Christian event corresponds to a freedom open to transcendence—the gift that is God himself. Although hidden, not only does God not demean human beings, but God actually lifts them up, setting them forth upon the path to the fullness of life, of joy, and of peace. Human freedom has nothing to fear from the proclamation of the gospel, for the good news of Christ Risen bears with it only our good, and the deliverance of freedom from every shape and form of slavery. Just so, membership in the Church does not coincide with the boundaries of the visible Church. Yet it cannot be "disconnected" from the Church, since it is "the efficacious sign of that Kingdom" and therefore is "the bearer of the presence of God and thus the instrument of the true humanization of man and the world"

56

(*Note*, 9). Further, inasmuch as evangelization is promoted with a method respectful of others' consciences and with a style of sincere dialogue, it cannot be interpreted as "proselytism," although it does imply testimonial and explicit proclamation, so that, ecumenically as well, one can arrive at full truth, and come to full truth and unity in truth and in love (cf. *Note*, 11).

Then, what stands behind the daily difficulties of evangelization, which can render believers so *perplexed* when confronted with the Lord's mandate of mission, and thus so *little creative* in the fundamental task of inculturating the gospel?

There exists a global crisis of context. The postmodern condition holds that it is impossible to tell the truth in human dialogue: truth is either nonexistent or unknowable. Relativism and agnosticism support very diffuse styles of thought, while an individualistic (and anarchical) conceptualization of liberty as indifference bids fair to carry the day.

In this climate, the effort of dialogue is understood as a necessary "enfeeblement" of the actual positing of truth: you have to dialogue without being able to say what you really think, lest, by not seeming to remain neutral, you exacerbate the potential for less than amicable confrontations. This has serious repercussions for evangelization, posing many a challenge, beginning with that of religious pluralism—"not only *de facto* but also *de jure* (or in principle)" (*Note*, 10) —threatening the Christian claim to proclaim Jesus Christ as the single and absolute mediator of salvation for human beings. The challenges can, however, translate into great opportunities and constitute a *kairos* for the faith, if Christians will only avail themselves of the swelling, limpid waters of their foundational experience: "Flowing into this self-critique of the modern age there also has to be a self-critique of modern Christianity, which must constantly renew its self-understanding setting out from its roots" (*Spe salvi*, 22).

# EVANGELIZATION AS "CONVERSION" IN THE CULTURES

Christian love is God's love planting itself amid the roots like water on parched soil, which can heal and rescue, for it is God's love for us. And so the connection between evangelization and promotion, development and human deliverance, is natural, and interior, for reasons anthropological, theological, and evangelical. This connection—the fundamental basis of the Church's salubrious cooperation with the Church vis-à-vis the problems of society—postulates a true assimilation of Christ, a better-than-superficial knowledge of the gospel, the defeat of the "divorce" between faith and life, in order to recover a needed Christian sensitivity in the face of the anxieties, not to say the anguish, of the human being today. In this way a person is able to light up the steps of her and his way, their hopes, and to be positive agents of the building of the future. Evangelization is not done for decorative reasons, but for in-depth and substantial purposes. It is also a matter of, through the might of the gospel, "affecting and as it were upsetting, through the power of the Gospel, mankind's criteria of judgment, determining values, points of interest, lines of thought, sources of inspiration and models of life, which are in contrast with the Word of God and the plan of salvation" (*Evangelii nuntiandi*, 19). The inculturation of the gospel points the way to the humanization of what is human in the human being, even when its preaching at times clashes with certain customs (*mores*) and even with particular cultural and historico-social situations.

What is needed is a "conversion" of the cultures to the faith with the proviso that the truths of the gospel remain interior to each culture, carrying them all to their most complete human development. The inculturation of the gospel is not only an "adaptation" of God's word to the cultures, but also, ineluctably, a "believing translation" of the cultures encountered. The *Doctrinal Note* asserts: "Although the Gospel is independent [of] any culture, it is capable of infusing all cultures, while never allowing itself to be subservient to them" (6). The believing translation of culture sometimes takes the shape of a great "helter-skelter from within" that always leads to the splendor of the human loveliness of every culture, despite the fact that at first glance it might as well be comporting rejections, and precise transformations.

A beautiful metaphor may help to grasp all of this. It is that of the "sycamore farmer" pointed out by Cardinal Joseph Ratzinger in his intervention, "Fare Cultura nel

Tempo della Communicazione" ("Building Culture in the Times of Communication," Rome, November 7–9, 2002). After all, "Christian faith is open to all that there is of grand, true, and pure in world culture," and "knows and seeks out the points of contact, recovers what there is of good, in opposition to whatever, in the cultures, bars the doors to the Gospel." It is needful that becoming Christian establishes "a vital rapport that will be able to realize the healthy recovery, and transformation, of culture." Every culture is like the sycamore tree, "a tree that produces a great deal of fruit. But this tree can have no flavor, unless it is pierced at the correct time and in correct manner, and kept from blooming and bearing before its time so that it may ripen and become pure, and not only promising but good."

Now, "the very *Logos* must impinge upon our culture and its fruits, so that what has been fertile will come to be purified, and not only fertile, but good....[Now,] granted, it is ultimately but the *Logos* himself that can lead our cultures to their authentic purity and maturity." But the *Logos* has need of its attendants, the "sycamore farmers." And that is not a thing that can happen in an instant. It is something that has need of continuous and convinced labor in the work and deed of evangelization. Yes, it requires the explicit proclamation, and the incarnation of this proclamation in concrete lifestyles and behaviors. That is, as the *Doctrinal Note* would have us remember, it calls for the "personal witness which is always very effective in spreading the Gospel" (11). After all, Christianity is mainly the presence of Christ in the world, in men and women in action. It is the real presence of God in the heart of the human being by way of the Spirit, who, as the *Doctrinal Note* reminds us, is "the principal agent of the inculturation of the Gospel" (6). Christianity is the good form of life. It is the form of life according to faith, hope, and charity. In evangelization the theological dimension of the Christian experience must never be forgotten.

# EVANGELIZATION, FREEDOM OF CONSCIENCE, AND RELIGIOUS FREEDOM

## Francesco Maceri

The recent *Doctrinal Note on Some Aspects of Evangelization* of the Congregation for the Doctrine of the Faith seeks to clarify the relationship between the duty of believers to assist human beings, with word and witness, in an encounter with Christ, in faith and respect for the conscience and religious freedom of all.[1] Because of a growing confusion, "often it is maintained that any attempt to convince others on religious matters is a limitation of their freedom....It would only be legitimate to present one's own ideas and to invite people to act according to their consciences, without aiming at their conversion to Christ and to the Catholic faith" (*Note*, 3).

Whence comes an enfeeblement of the missionary *élan*, whether "in favor of those who do not know" Christ, or "in favor of those who no longer follow Christian practice" (*Note*, 3). At bottom, the "confusion" is of a christological order. It regards the identity and salvific mediation of the Incarnate Son, the obfuscation of the inalienable Christian truth that "the world's redemption is the presence of the fullness of justice in a human Heart: in the heart of the Firstborn Son, that this may become justice in the hearts of many persons, who have been predestined from all eternity, precisely in the Firstborn Son, to become sons of God."[2] "The entire heart of man awaits the encounter with Jesus Christ" (*Note*, 10).

The confusion invests even the ecumenical task. The dimensions of listening, of dialogue that would be respectful of truth, charity, theological discussion are separated from that "witness and proclamation of elements which are not particular traditions or theological subtleties, but which belong rather to the Tradition of the faith itself" (*Note*, 12).

Gathering and developing some of the content and some of the argumentation of the *Note* in the perspective opened by such truths, we should like to show why authentic respect for conscience on the part of *believers in Christ* not only is no obstacle to the explicit proclamation of the gospel, but actually calls for it.

First of all, it is necessary to indicate what the nature of conscience is, in order to understand its authentic signification and the concrete requirements of the respect which is its due. With the term "moral conscience," Vatican II has designated a complex reality: no longer in the first instance the "voice" of a moral order, expressing the necessary relationships of human beings among themselves and their rapport with God, after the manner of the relations of necessity of impersonal creatures among themselves and with the Creator, but now God's messenger, for inner illumination. In the light of the whole content of the first chapter, *De humanae personae dignitate*, of the first part of the Pastoral Constitution *Gaudium et spes*, it must be asserted that, for Vatican II, conscience indicates the very person, one's own self, with his or her own activity and personal dynamism. It indicates the person's interiority, in whose depths that person encounters God, maintains a dialogue with God, and becomes aware of her or his essential orientation to the good and its transcendence. Conscience can be understood in its fullness only within the basic anthropological-christological coordinates taught by the Council: the Incarnate Son of God, who died and was glorified, is the key, center, and term of the whole of human history. In creation the human person receives from God a summons, definitively answered in Christ in such wise that in him alone is discovered the definitive profile of the original human calling—a call met in human beings through the work of the Holy Spirit in the Church, that sacrament of Christ and mystery of communion, and in dialogue with all human beings.[3] Conscience, therefore, comes forward with traits of a personalistic, christological, ecclesial nature, and one of openness to others. And these characteristics are inseparably joined, because of Christ. Alpha and Omega, Head and Body, he is both wellspring and pinnacle of all creatures, whether on the plane of creation or on that of redemption

and sanctification (cf. Col 1:15–20; Eph 1:3–23). It follows that the moral conscience, the most secret nucleus
and *sacrarium* of the human being, is to be considered and
understood in the bond of a provenance and destination
with the mystery of Christ. John Henry Cardinal Newman
had developed his own keen awareness of this necessity,
and expresses it quite clearly:

> The conscience is not self-blindness or selfish-
> ness, nor a desire to be self-consistent, but His
> messenger Who, be it in the world of nature or
> in that of grace, speaks to us from behind a veil,
> and instructs and governs us by means of his
> representatives. The conscience is the original
> vicar of Christ, prophetic in its words, sovereign
> in its peremptoriness, priestly in its benedic-
> tions and in its anathemas.[4]

Full respect for conscience comports with an
acknowledgment and high regard for its true nature.
Conscience is the inner place of the inchoate presence and
original representation of Christ Prophet, King, and Priest.
These are explained by the fact that the human being
bears, within, the imprint of the eternal and living law of
truth and perfection, of the image of the inaccessible
attributes of God, of the splendor of the Son,[5] and of the
everlasting love that has predestined him and her to be the
adopted children of God.[6] The gospel therefore corresponds to the actual nature of conscience. It is possessed of

an energy that allows it to enter into a profound rapport with the conscience, to strike a profound harmony with it.[7] The law we discover in the interior of our conscience, a law not ours to acquire but that must be obeyed, and that ever summons us to do and love the good and to flee evil,[8] finds Christ be it "the true 'complement'" that "realizes its authentic meaning with the total gift of self," or be it the one who, "by way of the Spirit, gives the grace of sharing his or her very life or very love."[9] Evangelization constitutes no form of prevarication on freedom of conscience. One who proclaims the gospel imposes nothing, but "points out," reveals, the One who, from all eternity, in the conscience, has been present but not known, heard but not identified, sought but not manifestly discerned. And so there comes a call, either to the individual, to recognize and accept being summoned by an "I," or else to others, for aid in that individual's progress in maturation, and in the fulfillment of his/her gift of "potential."

Up to this point in our essay, we have been attempting to show the legitimacy and appropriateness of a proclamation of the gospel in a perspective of the personal and christological characteristics of moral consciousness, or conscience, which Vatican II has assisted us to discover. Now we wish to show the correlation between evangelization and the awakening of moral consciousness.

We do not, with this reflection, seek to shirk our considerations vis-à-vis the *Doctrinal Note*. Actually retaining our central perspective of conscience, we turn our attention only to certain anthropological truths expressed in that document. We refer especially to this asseveration:

> Whoever trusts only in his own individual efforts and does not recognize the need for help from others, is deceiving himself....The need to trust in the knowledge handed on by one's culture or acquired by others, enriches a person with truths that could not have been attained on one's own, as well as by the interpersonal and social relationships which this process develops. (*Note*, 5)

Recalling all that the Council has taught, one must assert that the quest for truth, if it is to be carried on in a manner answering to the social nature of the human being, will be conducted not only with the faculties of the intellect and the will but also, and especially, by way of conscience.

The human person learns and recognizes the imperatives of the divine law by way of his or her conscience, which one is bound faithfully to follow in one's every activity, if one is to attain to one's end and purpose, God.[10]

In "fidelity to conscience," irrespective of our faith, language, and culture, we are impelled to dialogue among ourselves and to unity, while also being driven along a quest for truth—impelled also to resolve, in accordance with truth, so many moral problems in our lives. Naturally these provoke our anxiety, not to say anguish, individually and socially. As a consequence, "the communication of religiously significant events and truths in order that they will be accepted by others" (*Note*, 7) cannot be regarded as an expression of some want of esteem for conscience, but rather is a sign of complete respect for the attitude of others in their quest for solutions to the most profound questions arising from particular hearts, from the variety of cultures, and from the diversity of persons and their problems. Evangelization is in consonance with the human exigency to shape one's conscience aright. It may be objected that what is to be avoided is not so much the proposal, per se, of what is regarded by one's interlocutors as being true, as it is the prefatory conviction that may represent the actual scope of their intervention. This criticism implies an antecedent comprehension of the profound reality of evangelization. Evangelization is the living communication of one's own experience of Christ in faith. It is in the nature of this salvation encounter that the heart favored with it fairly kindles with a love of neighbor that moves it to give back disinterestedly what has been gratuitously had! One who sets forth to others the good news received and welcomed in faith feels filled with the urgency, the thrust, the glad burden, of the missionary mandate, and experiences the impossibility of estranging his or her own salvation from a procurement of the same for others (cf. 1 Cor 15:1–3; 1 John 1:1–4).

The Church does not regard God's mercy as an exclusive privilege, nor does the greatness of the privilege it enjoys make it feel unconcerned for those who do not share it. On the contrary, it finds in its own salvation an argument for showing more concern and more love for those who live close at hand, or to whom it can go in its endeavor to make all alike share the blessing of salvation.[11]

There is nothing presumptuous or aggressive in the enterprise of evangelization, even though the good it secures does correspond to anthropological reality (cf. *Note*, 7).

The *Doctrinal Note* also broaches a reflection on the profit of evangelization to the conscience of its protagonists. "Evangelization does not only entail the possibility of enrichment for those who are evangelized; it is also an enrichment for the one who does the evangelizing, as well as for the entire Church" (6).

By placing the gospel in dialogue with the positive and negative elements of the cultures, the Church can engage potentialities of the gospel little at hand until now, which will enrich the life of Christians and the Church (cf. *Note*, 6). None of this is strange to the conscience of the believer. The dialogue of truth and charity opens that conscience to the center of its Christian value and meaning, contributes to its formation, and renders it the still more transparent venue of the encounter with the Trinity: with the Father, the fountain of thoughts, of the prime elements of every being, and of its goodness; with the Son, in whom and for whom all has been created, and who is in our midst with a presence more glorious and mighty than when he was visible on earth; and with the Holy Spirit, who completes, in the variety of human situations, the design of the Father now perfected forever in the Son. Further, by sharing in the work of evangelization, the conscience of the believer shares in the task of the Church to "scrutinize the signs of the times and to interpret them in the light of the gospel" in order to "discern, in the requests and in the aspirations, in which it takes part along with the other human beings of our time, what the true signs are of God's presence or plan."[12] In this way its ecclesial dimension is reinforced and enriched.

Finally, as to ecumenical dimensions, the *Doctrinal Note* points out that, with the exclusion of any undue pressure and dishonest solicitation, "if a non-Catholic Christian, for reasons of conscience and having been convinced of Catholic truth, asks to enter into the full communion of the Catholic Church, this is to be respected as the work of the Holy Spirit and as an expression of freedom of conscience and of religion" (12). In the activity of evangelization, deception, selfish interests, and arrogance can accompany, or even replace, the original force of the divine will of the salvation of all. In this way, matters can come to serious disrespect for the dignity and conscience of others (cf. *Note*, 8).

This has actually occurred in history. The manifold transgressions and faults of the past ought to give life, in today's believers, not to a problematic sense of guilt but to a sense of sin. The former is conducive to a low appraisal of evangelization, the latter to contrition and to an experience of the merciful love of God that renews the heart, and transforms the sinner into an ardent missioner. "Against you, you alone, have I sinned…wash me, and I shall be whiter than snow…I will teach transgressors your ways, and sinners will return to you" (Ps 51:4, 7, 13). The evangelizer is a sinner reconciled by God (2 Cor 4:1). An intimate awareness of this truth is the best guarantee of fidelity to the missionary mandate, united with the respect due the conscience.

# EVANGELIZATION, ECUMENISM, PROSELYTISM

### Fernando Ocáriz Braña

"Ever since its beginnings, the ecumenical movement has been closely connected with evangelization." With these words we have the opening of the brief Part IV, entitled "Some ecumenical implications," of the recent *Doctrinal Note on Some Aspects of Evangelization*, published by the Congregation for the Doctrine of the Faith.[1] In treating this close connection between evangelism and ecumenism, the *Doctrinal Note* would have us keep particularly present the irreplaceable function of personal freedom in acceptance of the faith and incorporation into the Church—whence, too, a clarification on the question of proselytism emerges.

## EVANGELIZATION AND ECUMENISM

The relationship between evangelization and ecumenism comes clear most of all in Jesus' prayer to the

73

Father for the unity of his disciples, precisely for the sake of the fecundity of the evangelizing mission: "so that the world may believe" (John 17:21). Indeed, division "damages the most sacred cause of preaching."[2] But there is another aspect of the relationship between evangelization and ecumenism, a symmetrical one, so to speak: evangelization for the achievement of Christian unity. As the *Doctrinal Note* recalls, among the various dimensions of the ecumenical task, we certainly must not ignore the "witness and proclamation of elements which are not particular traditions or theological subtleties, but which belong rather to the Tradition of the faith itself" (*Note*, 12). This proclamation and testimonial, then, is evangelization, since it is *traditio Evangelii.*

The universality of the Church's mission comports with the essential purpose that none be excluded from her apostolic horizon. Accordingly, apart from the *missio ad gentes*, evangelization in the broad sense is also all of the activity of strengthening the faith and the sacramental life of the Catholic faithful themselves, that is, whether pastoral activity (of the pastors with the faithful) or the multiform apostolic succor lent one another, once more, by the faithful themselves. Finally, evangelization includes the "testimonial and proclamation" borne forth by Catholics to Christians not in full communion with the Catholic Church.

In evangelization in countries where non-Catholic Christians live, especially in lands of ancient Christian tradition, "what is required is both a genuine respect for their

traditions and spiritual riches, and a sincere spirit of cooperation." This respect is such that, in the words of Louis
Bouyer, "we shall not ask our separated brethren that they
altogether renounce anything that is positive, authentic, in
their great religious institutions. Rather, we shall ask them
courageously to extract from it all its logic."[3] In fact, the
very delving to the depths of what our non-Catholic siblings already possess of the authentically Christian, in and
of itself, leads them into Catholic plenitude.[4] It is a matter
not of ignoring or side-stepping existing doctrinal differences, but of sharing our common bases, taken seriously,
evaluated in depth, and lived with intensity.

Thus is also realized the testimonial of fraternal charity
among Christians in the face of the atheism and relativism,
frequently spread by force, of many a land with deep
Christian roots. Besides, cooperation between Catholics
and non-Catholics in activities of human and social interest, impregnated with a Christian spirit, is itself a manner
of Christian testimonial, despite the limitations and fail-
ings of persons.

Surely "it is evident that, when individuals wish for
full Catholic communion, their preparation and reconcili-
ation is an undertaking which of its nature is distinct from
ecumenical action. But there is no opposition between the
two, since both proceed from the marvelous ways of God."[5]
Therefore "it needs also to be recalled that if a non-
Catholic Christian, for reasons of conscience, and having
been convinced of Catholic truth, asks to enter into the full
communion of the Catholic Church, this is to be respected

as the work of the Holy Spirit and as an expression of freedom of conscience and of religion." (*Note*, 12). At the same time, the *Doctrinal Note* recalls that, "everywhere and always, each Catholic has the right and the duty to give the witness and the full proclamation of his faith" (*Note*, 12). Of the said fullness the Catholic not only could and should furnish explanations, when a family member or friend so requests, but should also bear witness, at once simple and powerful, of her or his own Christian living.

It is a matter, not of asserting one's own convictions, nor of seeming to have the upper hand, but of authentic charity, a sincere love for God and for these brothers and sisters and friends, that they receive the inestimable good of the fullness of the faith and the means of salvation. Indeed, as Pope Benedict XVI writes, "the love of God is revealed in responsibility for the other."[6] This apostolic task—of evangelization in the broad sense—is realized especially in the context of a true friendship, where "sincere and fraternal dialogue generates trust and confidence, eliminates fear and preconceptions, banishes difficulties, and opens up to serene and constructive comparison."[7]

Respect for everyone's freedom is not a tactic. It is a demand of justice and love. Precisely for this reason, and because of the relationship obtaining between freedom and truth, it not only does not exclude, but rather demands, the testimonial of one's own Christian conduct, as well as making known to one's friend the treasure of one's faith in the manner and measure in which that friend might desire it. On the other hand, the same loyalty to another will preclude any false pretense of doctrinal agreement when the latter is not really present.[8] "Love and witnessing to the truth are aimed above all at convincing others through the power of the word of God....The Christian mission resides in the power of the Holy Spirit and in the truth itself which is proclaimed" (*Note*, 12).

# THE QUESTION OF PROSELYTISM

The word *proselytism* occurs only once in the *Doctrinal Note*, being employed there in order to make it clear that, out of respect for the work of the Holy Spirit, "if a non-Catholic Christian...asks to enter into the full communion of the Catholic Church,...[i]n such a case it would not be a question of proselytism in the negative sense that has been attributed to this term" (*Note*, 12). Then a brief allusion in a footnote is made to the original, positive meaning of the word *proselytism*, and to the fact that only recently has it acquired a negative meaning, "the promotion of a religion by using means, and for motives, contrary to the spirit of the Gospel; that is, which do not safeguard the freedom and dignity of the human person. It is in this sense that the term proselytism is understood in the context of the ecumenical movement" (*Note*, endnote 49).

As we have observed—and the *Doctrinal Note* registers it as well—the word *proselytism* emerges from the Jewish cultural context. It is the Greek translation of the Hebrew *gēr* and occurs frequently in the Septuagint. It refers mainly to the foreigner who had stable abode in the Hebrew community and had the same rights and duties as the Hebrews themselves.[9]

The term is found only four times in the New Testament, once in Saint Matthew (Matt 23:15) and thrice in the Acts of the Apostles (Acts 2:11; 6:5; 13:43). It is in the text of Matthew that its denotation and connotations are most clearly expressed. Here it is quite clear that the reproach Jesus addresses to the scribes and Pharisees refers not to the fact that they sought to make proselytes but to their manner of doing so, and to the fact that they thereupon rendered the proselyte a "son of Gehenna" like themselves.[10]

The term then passed into the Christian tradition as the *Doctrinal Note* also recalls: "In the Christian context, the term proselytism was often used as a synonym for missionary activity" (*Note*, endnote 49), maintaining, then, its original positive meaning. The negative sense recently attributed to this term can be regarded as now prevalent in some languages, indeed in some contexts simply and exclusively, as with the ecumenical movement of our day. In other contexts, however, its original positive meaning prevails, even in civil contexts—juridical and political—where proselytism, obviously in its positive meaning, is acknowledged as an intrinsic component of religious freedom.[11] But this is not the matter—of a linguistic nature—that the *Doctrinal Note* has sought to clarify.

The *Doctrinal Note* wishes to make a different clarification: one should not call proselytism, understood in a

negative sense, that which is in truth a form of evangelization (what one might call a form of proselytism in the original sense of the word). Thus, the clarification is not a
superfluous one. It is not infrequent today to hear the word
*proselytism* (in the negative sense) used as a description of
the missionary task,[12] a trend that has a great deal to do with
that "dictatorship of relativism that acknowledges nothing
as definitive, leaving as ultimate measure only the ego and
its volitions."[13] More concretely, in the context of ecumenism, it cannot be considered blameworthy to accompany non-Catholic Christians, by the witness and
proclamation of one's own faith, along the pathway of their
free desire for full incorporation into the Church.

And so, on the very day of the publication of the
*Doctrinal Note*, the secretary of the Congregation for the
Doctrine of the Faith pronounced: "In any case, the right
and responsibility to proclaim, in fullness, one's own faith
is recognized for all, including Catholics with regard to
other Christians who freely elect to receive it. To reject
this would mean to deny a fundamental human right."[14]
Naturally, this is to be done always and everywhere with
the utmost respect for and defense of the intimacy and
freedom of persons. "We impose our faith on no one. A
proselytism of that sort is contrary to Christianity. The
faith can develop only in freedom."[15]

In conclusion: It emerges from the *Doctrinal Note*
with renewed clarity that nothing could justify the claim
that the Church ought to renounce the universality of her
mission. Indeed, ever to be open to the missionary and

ecumenical dynamic appertains to her nature, sent as she is to the world to gather everyone and everything together in Christ,[16] and thus to constitute, according to the will of the Lord, one flock, one shepherd (cf. John 10:16).

Surely, in the various dimensions of ecumenism, institutional and individual, the obstacles are great. Yet there is always room for prayer and dialogue, hoping in the action of the Holy Spirit. And, at the same time, a pressing need remains for "that 'purification of the memory,' so many times evoked by Pope John Paul II, that alone can dispose minds and hearts to receive the full truth of Christ."[17]

# Notes

## Document: *Doctrinal Note on Some Aspects of Evangelization*

1. John Paul II, Encyclical Letter *Redemptoris missio* (7 December 1990), 47: AAS [*Acta Apostolicae Sedis*] 83 (1991), 293.

2. Second Vatican Council, Dogmatic Constitution *Lumen gentium*, 14; cf. Decree *Ad gentes*, 7; Decree *Unitatis redintegratio*, 3. This teaching does not contradict the universal salvific will of God, who "desires everyone to be saved and to come to the knowledge of the truth" (1 Tim 2:4); therefore, "it is necessary to keep these two truths together, namely, the real possibility of salvation in Christ for all mankind and the necessity of the Church for salvation" (John Paul II, Encyclical Letter *Redemptoris missio*, 9: AAS 83 [1991], 258).

3. Cf. John Paul II, Apostolic Letter *Novo millennio ineunte* (6 January 2001), 1: AAS 93 (2001), 266.

4. Cf. Paul VI, Apostolic Exhortation *Evangelii nuntiandi* (8 December 1975), 24: AAS 69 (1976), 22.

5. John Paul II, Encyclical Letter *Redemptoris missio*, 46: AAS 83 (1991), 293; cf. Paul VI, Apostolic

Exhortation *Evangelii nuntiandi,* 53 and 80: AAS 69 (1976), 41–42, 73–74.

6. Benedict XVI, *Homily at the Mass celebrated at the outdoor site of the Neue Messe in Munich* (10 September 2006): AAS 98 (2006), 710.

7. Saint Thomas Aquinas, *Summa Theologiae,* I–II, q. 109, a.1, ad 1: "any truth, no matter by whom it is spoken, is from the Holy Spirit."

8. Cf. John Paul II, Encyclical Letter *Fides et ratio* (14 September 1998), 44: AAS 91 (1999), 40.

9. Benedict XVI, *Address to the Participants in the Ecclesial Diocesan Convention of Rome "Family and Christian community: formation of the person and transmission of the faith"* (6 June 2005): AAS 97 (2005), 816.

10. John Paul II, Encyclical Letter *Fides et ratio,* 5: AAS 91 (1999), 9–10.

11. *Ibidem,* 31: AAS 91 (1999), 29; cf. Second Vatican Council, Pastoral Constitution *Gaudium et spes,*12.

12. This right was recognized and affirmed also by the *Universal Declaration of Human Rights of 1948* (art. 18–19).

13. John Paul II, Encyclical Letter *Fides et ratio,* 33: AAS 91 (1999), 31.

14. Second Vatican Council, Dogmatic Constitution *Dei Verbum,* 5.

15. Second Vatican Council, Declaration *Dignitatis humanae,* 3.

16. *Ibidem,* 1.

17. John Paul II, Encyclical Letter *Redemptoris missio*, 52: AAS 83 (1991), 300.

18. Cf. John Paul II, Encyclical Letter *Slavorum Apostoli* (2 June 1985), 18: AAS 77 (1985), 800.

19. Second Vatican Council, Dogmatic Constitution *Dei Verbum*, 8.

20. Cf. Paul VI, Apostolic Exhortation *Evangelii nuntiandi*, 19–20: AAS 69 (1976), 18–19.

21. Second Vatican Council, Decree *Ad gentes*, 7; cf. Dogmatic Constitution *Lumen gentium*, 16; Pastoral Constitution *Gaudium et spes*, 22.

22. Benedict XVI, *Homily at the Mass for the Inauguration of the Pontificate* (24 April 2005): AAS 97 (2005), 711.

23. Cf. First Vatican Council, Dogmatic Constitution *Dei Filius*, 2: "It is indeed thanks to this divine revelation, that those matters concerning God, which are not of themselves beyond the scope of human reason, can, even in the present condition of the human race, be known by everyone without difficulty, with firm certitude and with no admixture of error (cf. Saint Thomas Aquinas, *Summa Theologiae*, I, q.1, a.1)" (DH 3005).

24. Second Vatican Council, Decree *Ad gentes*, 13.

25. Second Vatican Council, Declaration *Dignitatis humanae*, 11.

26. Cf., for example, Clement of Alexandria, *Protrepticus* (*Exhortation to the Greeks*), IX, 87, 3–4 (Sources Chrétiennes 2:154–155); Saint Augustine,

Sermo 14D [=352 A], 3 (*Nuova Biblioteca Agostiniana,* XXXV/1, 269–271).

27. Second Vatican Council, Dogmatic Constitution *Lumen gentium,* 5.

28. Cf. John Paul II, Encyclical Letter *Redemptoris missio,* 18: AAS 83 (1991), 265–266: "If the kingdom is separated from Jesus, it is no longer the kingdom of God which he revealed. The result is a distortion of the meaning of the kingdom, which runs the risk of being transformed into a purely human or ideological goal, and a distortion of the identity of Christ, who no longer appears as the Lord to whom everything must one day be subjected (cf. 1 Cor 15:27)."

29. John Paul II, Encyclical Letter *Redemptoris missio,* 18: AAS 83 (1991), 266. On the relationship between Christ and the Kingdom, cf. also Congregation for the Doctrine of the Faith, Declaration *Dominus Iesus* (6 August 2000), 18–19: AAS 92 (2000), 759–761.

30. Congregation for the Doctrine of the Faith, Declaration *Dominus Iesus,* 4: AAS 92 (2000), 744.

31. Cf. Paul VI, Apostolic Exhortation *Evangelii nuntiandi,* 80: AAS 69 (1976), 73: "Besides, it is added, why proclaim the Gospel when the whole world is saved by uprightness of heart? We know likewise that the world and history are filled with "seeds of the Word"; is it not therefore an illusion to claim to bring the Gospel where it already exists in the seeds that the Lord Himself has sown?"

32. Cf. Benedict XVI, *Address to the Roman Curia offering Christmas Greetings* (22 December 2005): AAS 98

(2006), 50: "…if religious freedom were to be considered an expression of the human inability to discover the truth and thus become a canonization of relativism, then this social and historical necessity is raised inappropriately to the metaphysical level and thus stripped of its true meaning. Consequently, it cannot be accepted by those who believe that the human person is capable of knowing the truth about God and, on the basis of the inner dignity of the truth, is bound to this knowledge. It is quite different, on the other hand, to perceive religious freedom as a need that derives from human coexistence, or indeed, as an intrinsic consequence of the truth that cannot be externally imposed but that the person must adopt only through the process of conviction."

33. Second Vatican Council, Pastoral Constitution *Gaudium et spes*, 28; cf. Paul VI, Apostolic Exhortation *Evangelii nuntiandi*, 24: AAS 69 (1976), 21–22.

34. Cf. John Paul II, Encyclical Letter *Redemptoris missio*, 21–30: AAS 83 (1991), 268–276.

35. Benedict XVI, *Homily at the Mass for the Inauguration of the Pontificate* (24 April 2005): AAS 97 (2005), 710.

36. *Ibidem.*

37. Cf. Second Vatican Council, Declaration *Dignitatis humanae*, 6.

38. Indeed, where the right to religious freedom is recognized, the right to share one's own convictions with others in full respect for their consciences is usually recognized as well; this sharing is aimed at having others enter one's own

religious community and is an established right in numerous legal systems, with a well-developed jurisprudence.

39. Cf. Dante Alighieri, *La Divina Commedia: Paradiso*, 33:87: "che per l'universo si squaderna."

40. Paul VI, Apostolic Exhortation *Evangelii nuntiandi*, 46: AAS 69 (1976), 36.

41. Cf. Second Vatican Council, Dogmatic Constitution *Lumen gentium*, 35.

42. Paul VI, Apostolic Exhortation *Evangelii nuntiandi*, 22: AAS 69 (1976), 20.

43. Second Vatican Council, Decree *Unitatis redintegratio*, 1; cf. John Paul II, Encyclical Letter *Redemptoris missio*, 1 and 50: AAS 83 (1991), 249, 297.

44. Cf. John Paul II, Encyclical Letter *Redemptoris missio*, 34: AAS 83 (1991), 279–280.

45. Second Vatican Council, Decree *Ad gentes*, 15.

46. John Paul II, Encyclical Letter *Ut unum sint* (25 May 1995), 14: AAS 87 (1995), 929.

47. Cf. *ibidem*, 28: AAS 87 (1995), 939.

48. Cf. Second Vatican Council, Decree *Unitatis redintegratio*, 3 and 5.

49. The term *proselytism* originated in the context of Judaism, in which the term *proselyte* referred to someone who, coming from the gentiles, had passed into the Chosen People. So too, in the Christian context, the term proselytism was often used as a synonym for missionary activity. More recently, however, the term has taken on a negative connotation, to mean the promotion of a religion by using means, and for motives, contrary to the spirit of

the Gospel; that is, which do not safeguard the freedom and dignity of the human person. It is in this sense that the term proselytism is understood in the context of the ecumenical movement: cf. *The Joint Working Group between the Catholic Church and the World Council of Churches*, "The Challenge of Proselytism and the Calling to Common Witness" (1995).

50. Second Vatican Council, Decree *Unitatis redintegratio*, 4.

51. Second Vatican Council, Declaration *Dignitatis humanae*, 4.

52. Cf. Benedict XVI, Encyclical Letter *Deus caritas est* (25 December 2005), 31 c: AAS 98 (2006), 245.

53. Cf. Second Vatican Council, Declaration *Dignitatis humanae*, 11.

54. Benedict XVI, *Homily during the visit to the Basilica of Saint Paul outside the Walls* (25 April 2005): AAS 97 (2005), 745.

55. Benedict XVI, *Address to the participants in the International Conference on the 40th anniversary of the conciliar Decree "Ad gentes"* (11 March 2006): AAS 98 (2006), 334.

56. Benedict XVI, Encyclical Letter *Deus caritas est*, 18: AAS 98 (2006), 232.

## SECOND COMMENT: THE ECCLESIOLOGICAL PRESUPPOSITIONS OF EVANGELIZATION

1. Congregation for the Doctrine of Faith, Decree *Dominus Iesus*, 18.

2. Shedding further light on the observation by John Paul II, in his Encyclical Letter *Redemptoris missio*, 19, sub fine: "Paul VI, who has asserted 'the existence of a profound bond connecting Christ, the Church, and evangelization,' has also said that the Church 'is not an end in herself, but fervently seeks to be altogether of Christ, in Christ, and for Christ, and altogether of human beings, among human beings, and for human beings.'"

3. For this conception and its risks, see the lucid passage in *Redemptoris missio*, 17.

4. Among the observations in the *Doctrinal Note*, one can read the following citation from *Redemptoris missio*,18: "The kingdom of God is not a concept, a doctrine, or a program subject to free interpretation, but it is before all else *a person* with the face and name of Jesus of Nazareth, the image of the invisible God."

5. For this meaning of the axiom, see International Theological Commission, *Christianity and the Religions*. The sense is expressed in *Redemptoris missio*, 18: "Christ has bestowed on the Church, his body, the fullness of the goods and means of salvation."

6. See Joseph Ratzinger, *Fede, verità, tolleranza: Il*

*cristianesimo e le religione del mondo* [*Faith, Truth, Tolerance: Christianity and the Religions of the World*] (Siena: Cantagalli, 2003), 65–67.

7. Ibid., 205.

8. Ibid., 210–211.

9. Ibid., 91–92.

# FOURTH COMMENT: EVANGELIZATION, FREEDOM OF CONSCIENCE, AND RELIGIOUS FREEDOM

1. In the reflections to follow, we consider freedom of and respect for the conscience, inasmuch as religious liberty is a special case of the two. The supreme exercise of the freedom with which human beings seek, spontaneously, their Creator, and tend toward their end with free choice of the good (*Gaudium et spes*, 17; 1/1370), is rooted in the depths of conscience, where a person is alone with God, has the experience of her/his charity, and thereby discovers the law of love of God and neighbor. The dignity and authenticity of the freedom of the person are at stake in conscience, since this is where the original encounter occurs with God and with Christ, and upon its rightness depends the distancing of every act of will (cf. *Gaudium et spes*, 16; 1/1369).

2. John Paul II, Encyclical Letter *Redemptor hominis*, 9. We have chosen this text because the most radical and burning doubt regards precisely salvific truth, a

phenomenon that invests the whole person, and not merely truth as an object of thought. Cf. ibid., 4.

3. See Vatican Council II, Pastoral Constitution *Gaudium et spes*, 22.

4. John Henry Newman, *A Letter Addressed to His Grace the Duke of Norfolk on Occasion of Mr. Gladstone's Recent Expostulation of 1874* (London, 1875). For Newman, the One speaking to us by way of conscience is the Legislator and the Redeemer, who instructs us and guides us by way of his visible representatives. Being *solus cum Solo* in the interiority and depth of conscience does not isolate a person but disposes her or him to openness and receptivity, in God, to all things.

5. Newman, *Plain and Parochial Sermons* (San Francisco: Ignatius Press, 1997), 365.

6. The dynamic bond of origin and orientation of the human conscience with the Paschal mystery is the object of our contribution "La Coscienza Morale Filiale" ("The Filial Moral Conscience") in the tractate *Figli nel Figlio: Una Teologia Morale Fondamentale* ("Sons and Daughters in the Son: A Fundamental Moral Theology").

7. Paul VI, Apostolic Exhortation *Evangelii nuntiandi*, 4; 5/1591.

8. Cf. Vatican Council II, Pastoral Constitution *Gaudium et spes*, 16.

9. John Paul II, Encyclical Letter *Veritatis splendor*, 15.

10. Vatican Council II, Declaration *Dignitatis humanae*, 3.

11. Paul VI, Encyclical Letter *Ecclesiam suam*, 65.

12. Vatican Council II, Pastoral Constitution *Gaudium et spes*, 11.

# FIFTH COMMENT: EVANGELIZATION, ECUMENISM, PROSELYTISM

1. Congregation for the Doctrine of the Faith, *Doctrinal Note on Some Aspects of Evangelization* (December 3, 2007, 12). In what follows here, all citations whose indications are not expressly given in the notes are from the present Part IV, no. 12 (sole subdivision of *Doctrinal Note* in Part IV).

2. Vatican Council II, Decree *Unitatis redintegratio*, 1.

3. Louis Bouyer, *Parole, église et sacrements en le protestantisme et le catholicisme* (Bruges: Declée de Brouwer, 1960), 91–92.

4. Cf. Vatican Council II, Dogmatic Constitution *Lumen gentium*, 8; Decree *Unitatis redintegratio*, 3.

5. Vatican Council II, Decree *Unitatis redintegratio*, 4; cf. Pedro Rodríguez, *Iglesia y ecumenismo* (Madrid: Rialp, 1979), 87–88.

6. Benedict XVI, Encyclical Letter *Spe salvi*, 28.

7. Benedict XVI, "Address to the Participants at the Meeting of the Delegates of the Churches, the Bishops' Conferences, Communities, and Ecumenical Organisms of Europe" (January 26, 2006).

8. Cf. Vatican Council II, Decree *Unitatis redintegratio*, 11.

9. See K. G. Kuhn, "Prosélytos," in G. Kittel and G. Friedrich, *Grande Lessico del Nuovo Testamento* (Brescia: Paideia, 1980), 11:303 (Eng. trans.: *Theological Dictionary of the New Testament* [Grand Rapids: Eerdmans]).

10. See H. Kuhli, "Prosélytos," in H. Balz and G. Schneider, *Dizionario Esegetico del Nuovo Testamento* (Brescia: Paideia, 1998), 1151–54 (Eng. trans.: *Exegetical Dictionary of the New Testament* [Grand Rapids: Eerdmans, 1990)]. Hypotheses vary as to the causes of this "double" wickedness. See Ernst Lerle, *Proselytenwerbung und Urchistentum* (Berlin: Evangelische Verlagsanstalt, 1960), 64–65.

11. See, for example, Nicolas Sarkozy, *La république, les religions, l'espérance* (Paris: Cerf, 2004), 153.

12. Cf. John Paul II, Encyclical Letter *Redemptoris missio*, 46.

13. Joseph Ratzinger, "Homily at the Beginning of the Conclave" (April 18, 2005).

14. A. Amato, "Evangelizzazione rispetta e valoriza la libertà dell'altro," interview by F. M. Valiante in *L'Osservatore Romano* (December 15, 2007), 1.

15. Benedict XVI, Homily in Munich (September 10, 2006). Cf. Vatican Council II, Declaration *Dignitatis humanae*, 4; John Paul II, Encyclical Letter *Redemptoris missio*, 55.

16. Congregation for the Doctrine of the Faith, Letter *Communionis notio* (May 28, 1992), 4.

17. Benedict XVI, "Message Urbi et Orbi," April 20, 2005.

# CONTRIBUTORS

**Javier María Prades López** is a priest of the Archdiocese of Madrid (Spain) and Dean of the School of Theology of "St. Dámaso," also in Madrid. He is a member of the International Theological Commission. Among his publications are *"Deus specialiter est in sanctis per gratiam": El misterio de la inhabitación de la Trinidad, en los escritos de Santo Tomás* (Rome: Pontificia Università Gregoriana, 1993); *Dios ha salvado la distancia* (Madrid: Encuentro, 2003); *"Communicatio Christi": Reflexiones de teología sistemática* (Madrid, 2004); *Lietamente ti ho dato tutto* (Genoa-Milan, 2006); *La razón ¿enemiga del Misterio?* (Madrid, 2007); *Nostalgia di Resurrezione* (Siena, 2007); *Occidente: l'ineludibile incontro* (Siena, 2008). He has also edited or coedited fifteen other books and has written over fifty articles on theology.

**Alberto Cozzi** is a priest of the Archdiocese of Milan (Italy) and Professor of Theology at the Seminary of Milan and at the Theological Faculty of Northern Italy. He has published *Dio ha molti nomi* (Milan: Paoline, 1999); *La centralità di Cristo nella teologia di L. Billot* (Milan: Glossa, 1999); *Gesù Cristo tra le religioni: Mediatore dell'originario* (Assisi, 2004); *Conoscere Gesù nella fede. Un manuale di*

*Cristologia* (Assisi: Cittadella, 2007). He is author also of a number of theological articles.

**Antonio Staglianò** is Bishop of Noto (Italy) and has taught at the Theological Faculty of Southern Italy in Naples and the Institute of Religious Science of Crotone. He also taught theology at the Pontifical Gregorian University. He has published *Madre di Dio: La mariologia personalistica di Joseph Ratzinger* (Milan: San Paolo, 2010); *Teologia e spiritualità: pensiero critico ed esperienza cristiana* (Rome, 2006); *Ecce homo: la persona, l'idea di cultura e la questione antropologica in papa Wojtyla* (Siena: Cantagalli, 2008); *Intagliatori di sicomoro: cristianesimo ed emergenze culturali del terzo millennio: il compito, le sfide, gli orizzonti* (Catanzaro: Rubbettino, 2009); *L'identità meridionale: percorsi di riflessione teologica* (Milan: San Paolo, 2004); *Su due ali: l'impegno per la ragione, responsabilità della fede* (Rome: Lateran University Press, 2005); *Vangelo e comunicazione: radicare la fede nel nuovo millennio* (Bologna: EDB, 2001). He has also published a number of theological articles.

**Francesco Maceri** is a priest of the Society of Jesus and teaches at the Pontifical Theological Faculty of Sardinia and at the Institute of Religious Science of Cagliari (Italy). He has published *La formazione della coscienza del credente: Una proposta educativa alla luce dei "Parochial and Plain Sermons" di John Henry Newman* (Rome: Gregorian University Press, 2001); *John Henry Newman. Pellegrino della verità* (Cosenza: Progetto, 1993). He has also published a number of theological articles.

## Contributors

**Fernando Ocáriz Braña** is a priest and a consultor of the Congregation for the Doctrine of the Faith, as well as of the Pontifical Council for the New Evangelization. He has been a professor at the Pontifical University of the Holy Cross and has been a member of the Pontifical Theological Academy since 1989. He is the author of several books, including *Natura, grazia e gloria* (Roma, 2004); *Voltaire: Tratado sobre la tolerancia* (Madrid, 1980); *Amor a Dios. Amor a los hombres* (Madrid, 1979); and *Hijos de Dios en Cristo* (Pamplona, 1972). In addition, he has coauthored a number of books, including *Abba, Vater. Als Kinder Gottes Leben* (Köln, 1999); *Fundamental Theology* (Woodridge, IL, 2009); *Los laicos en la eclesiología del Concilio Vaticano II: santificar el mundo desde dentro* (Madrid, 2006); and *Rivelazione, fede e credibilità: Corso di teologia fondamentale* (Rome, 2001).